Ghost Train!

American Railroad Ghost Legends

as collected and retold by

Tony Reevy

1998
TLC Publishing Inc.
1387 Winding Creek Lane
Lynchburg, VA 24503-3776

Front Cover Illustration:
"Ghost Train" by Mark Harland Johnson

Back Cover Illustration:
"Ghost Train of the Arizona Desert" by Mark Harlan Johnson

© Copyright 1998
TLC Publishing, Inc.

Library of Congress Catalogue Card Number 98-61
ISBN 1-883089-41-7

Layout and Design by Kenneth L. Miller
Miller Design & Photography, Salem, Va.

Printed by
Walsworth Publishing Co.
Marceline, Mo. 64658

Table of Contents

Acknowledgements

America's railroad ghost legends are fading fast, victims of our transient, modern life style. Many of these stories would have vanished long ago if it wasn't for pioneering authors like Richard M. Dorson, Freeman Hubbard, Louis C. Jones, Ruth Ann Musick, and Nancy Roberts. My modest attempt to collect and retell railroad ghost stories really represents many other people's work. Folks who helped out by providing tales are recognized in the "Notes on the Sources" section of the book, and sources of illustrations are acknowledged in the photo captions.

John Hickman, a well-known rail enthusiast from the Washington, D. C. area, got it all started when he read an earlier manuscript and told me most of it had been done before; except for the ghost stories.

Many thanks also to the folks at the following periodicals who had faith in my articles about railroad ghosts: Managing Editor Scott Smith and the other fine folks at The State magazine here in North Carolina; the ever-helpful Frank G. Tatnall and his volunteer staff at National Railway Bulletin; and Leanne McGruder at Norfolk Southern's **Thoroughbred Paces**.

Melissa Ellis, former director of the Wilmington Railroad Museum in Wilmington, North Carolina, was kind enough to talk with me about the project—and the Maco Light—early on.

Bill Moose of Mitchell Community College (Statesville, North Carolina) did some research not acknowledged in the "Notes on the Sources."

Frank F. Raisig went above and beyond the call by

braving the ghost of Hannah Scott to take pictures of
the Ransomville, New York station; he later provided a
wonderful old photo of the building. My parents,
Carole and Bill Reevy of Durham, North Carolina,
helped by keeping an eye out for railroad ghost legends.

Most of all, I would like to thank my publisher, Tom
Dixon, for believing in my work; and my wife, Caroline
Weaver, for her patience. Many nights, I shut myself up
alone in our study while various revenants crowded
around my shoulders as I retold their stories; what's
more, the gremlins attracted by my writing about ghosts
and phantoms still lurk in her printer.

Many thanks to all of these folks, and to the railroaders who kept these stories alive down through the
years. I'm always interested in hearing about railroad
ghost stories I missed; readers may send them to me, if
the spirit moves them, care of TLC Publishing.

———————

—to Caroline—

Introduction

"Why, as to that, said the engineer,
Ghosts ain't things we are apt to fear;
Spirits don't fool with levers much,
And throttle-valves don't take to such;
And as for Jim,
What happened to him
Was one half fact, and t'other half whim!"

Bret Harte, "The Ghost That Jim Saw," c. 1882.

The ghost train is a common motif in railroad folklore. It is the "Flying Dutchman" of the rails, running on into folk history without end. A broader look at railroad folklore reveals many other ghostly manifestations associated with trains: ghostly lights; ghost whistles; ghosts walking, running, or standing along the way; hoodooed engines; haunted cabooses. All of these and more have been reported along America's railways.

It's a bewildering plenty of phantoms. In trying to group these legends together, I found six main categories of railroad ghost legends--and that's the way this book is organized. The first chapter focuses on ghost trains. Of all railroad specters, the ghost train has the strongest hold on the American imagination--the wheezing, clanking, old, steam train, staffed maybe by skeletons, creeping along a track somewhere in America. One of our most famous railroad ghost legends, that of Lincoln's Train, falls into this group of stories.

Closely related to ghost trains are the phantoms in the second chapter, which highlights ghostly wreck reenactments. Usually realistic, often appearing on the anniversary of the tragedy, ghostly wreck reenactment legends can usually be traced to an accident that actually occurred.

The Baltimore & Ohio Railroad, one of the nation's first railroads, also seems to be America's most haunted line. B&O behemoths like this 1845 vintage "mud digger," Cumberland, certainly suggest demons and ghost trains.

The most common category of railroad ghost legends, haunts along the tracks, is discussed in the third and fourth chapters. Haunts along the tracks may be divided into two main identifiable types—headless ghosts and ghostly lights—both of which are discussed in Chapter Three.   What is perhaps the most famous American railroad ghost—the Maco Light—shows up among the ghostly lights along the tracks. The remaining stories of ghosts along the tracks, grouped together for convenience's sake in Chapter Four, are a ghostly miscellany of shape-changing phantoms, ghostly music, ghostly mist, ghost tramps and more.

The fourth category is Chapter Five's haunted tunnels, the most famous of these being West Virginia's Big Bend Tunnel. Big Bend Tunnel is the place where John Henry reportedly worked, died, became a legend in song and story—and then returned from the dead.

The most interesting thing about the stories in the final two categories, haunted railroad stations and haunted rail cars, is how few of them there are. It is difficult to account for the lack of legends about haunted train stations, outlined here in Chapter Six. At first thought, it seems that haunted stations would be commonplace: after all, train stations were an important part of most American communities and have often survived to the present day. Yet they seem much less likely to be haunted than houses, for example. The only explanation that suggests itself is that they were rarely the scene of a fatality. Although train stations were often the settings of tragic personal events, seldom did anyone actually die in one. The release of psychic energy, whether actual or psychological, brought about by a death does seem to be what causes most hauntings.

In the case of rail cars, engines and rolling stock, discussed in Chapter Seven, the explanation for the dearth of legends is probably transience. The same passenger rarely sees the same sleeping car, for example, and that sleeper may only have a service life of twenty or thirty years. It's hard for ghost legends to form about an object that's always in motion, and that isn't visited by the same people on a regular basis.

Finally, what about the most interesting ghostly subject of all, the question that anyone studying ghosts is asked over and over again? We have to accept that, at least as things stand now, it is impossible to say whether ghosts really exist; whether any of these legends has a basis in observed fact. Perhaps we'll never know if ghosts are reported because they really manifest themselves or because people have a deep-set need to believe in the possibility of existence after death. The issue, of course, has been a subject of debate for centuries.

"It was cold and damp in the hobo camp
When a tired and hungry bo,
Fretfully slept as the shadows crept
On his bed in the sleet and snow.
As the cold wind whined, the hobo's mind
Fled back through the bygone years
When the rumbling strain of a fast train
Fell on his dreamy ears.

The semaphore dropped,
and the rattler stopped,
Midst the air brakes' shrieks and groans.
In the high cab chair, sitting there
Was the long dead Casey Jones.
She was a manifest and headed west,
And a hobo's dream of heaven.
On the engine's side the hobo spied,
The number Ninety-seven. "

Charles Blue, "The Phantom Drag."

This book does not try to answer any of these deep philosophical questions: it merely retells railroad ghost stories. Whatever the reason for their prominence, ghosts play a crucial role in our thought and legend. Not surprisingly, then, ghosts have become an important part of railroad folklore over the years, and railroad ghost stories are well worth studying on their own account.

Rather than analyzing and getting my thoughts in your way, I've chosen to assume that what the American people have said about these stories down through the years is true. This approach allows us to present America's railroad ghost legends, categorize them, and seek for the kernel of truth that tends to lie at the center of every piece of folklore. Some of the stories are famous, some of them are obscure, but all of them are redolent of coal smoke and signal oil, and of railroad days gone by.

I just hope you enjoy reading the stories as much as I enjoyed finding them.

The actual Lincoln's Funeral Train, with Pennsylvania Railroad No. 331, at West Philadelphia, Pennsylvania, April 22, 1865.

Ghost Trains

hen you think about railroad ghosts, what comes to mind is probably a story like this: A steam-engine-drawn ghost train clanking through the dark night, shining its headlight down little-used tracks and whistling for a vanished crossing.

While not the most common type of railroad ghost — haunts along the tracks take that title —the ghost train is the revenant most specifically associated with railroads. It certainly has won a strong place in American folklore, as the many recountings of the Lincoln's Train story in our ghost literature prove.

What causes a ghost train haunting? Usually, a train wreck or the death of a person struck by a train. Perhaps the most eerie ghost train stories, though, are the ones with no explanation. A ghost train runs through a desert that never saw a real railroad track, for example, or an engineer finds a terrible message scrawled on his frosty cab window. Weird, inexplicable stories like these are the most disturbing—and most interesting—of all.

Lincoln's Train

Every year at midnight on the evening of April 26 (or thereabouts), a chill wind runs down the tracks of Conrail's main line between New York City and Albany, a stretch of railroad that was once the Hudson Division of the New York Central System. If there is a moon, clouds slowly obscure it, and the air all about becomes still.

Railroad men who happen to be working then all step

aside and watch. They know what's going to happen, although any chance passersby are in for a surprise.

Soon, the men know for sure they are in the presence of the unknown. A black carpet seems to roll down the tracks, and all sound is deadened. Then, it comes: Lincoln's funeral train. The train, which crawls slowly by, is divided into two sections, both led by old-time, wood-burning engines with huge smokestacks, resplendent with polished brass. The engines are heavily draped in flowing black crepe.

The first section of the train is made up of an engine—running without a crew—that pulls several flat cars. On one of the flat cars is a grotesque band of skeletons sitting in fantastic poses, playing noiselessly on black instruments.

The first section is followed by the funeral train itself, which is made up of an engine pulling one flat car. On the flat car is a single lonely coffin, attended by neither ghost nor skeleton. As the train passes, ghosts of men in blue uniforms, some of them carrying their own coffins, may be seen floating in the air all around. Neither train makes a sound as it passes by.

If another train happens to go by at the same time as Lincoln's train, the ghostly train runs right through the real one without harming it. As it does so, the sounds made by the real train are muffled.

The next morning, all of the clocks on the old Hudson Division are unaccountably five to eight minutes behind. What's more, all of the trains that were out on the line the night before are running five to eight minutes late. The old-timers know why, though: Lincoln's funeral train stopped time as it ran by.

"The Warsaw Ghost Train"

Warsaw, North Carolina is a little country town located on CSX's rail lines. The railroad through Warsaw was once part of an Atlantic Coast Line route into Wilmington, North Carolina.

The Warsaw ghost train's story begins in November 1906, when an evening freight train's crew accidentally left a switch open on the main line. The open switch hadn't been discovered the next morning when the southbound passenger train whistled for Warsaw station.

See Special Notice on Page 2.

ROCKY MOUNT, WILMINGTON AND FLORENCE.

103	49	41	Mls	STATIONS.	102	48	42	
	P.M.	A.M.	P.M.			P.M.	P.M.	A.M.	
....	†3 58	*9 05	*7 25	....	Lv...**Richmond**..Ar.	1 00	8 00	5 10	
....	†8 05	*1 00	*5 27	0	" ...**Rocky Mt**⊙ "	8 50	2 05	11 15	
....	8 15	‖1 50	5 37	1	" **S. Rocky Mt**⊙ "	8 40	‖1 37	11 00	
....	f8 22	11 59	f5 45	5	" ..Sharpsburg...Lv.	f8 32	.....	f10 50	
....	†8 30	f2 07	f5 54	10	" .....Elm City..⊙ "	f8 25	f1 21	f10 40	
....	8 40	2 20	6 07	16	Ar. ....**Wilson**...⊙Lv.	8 13	1 07	10 25	
....	8 40	2 20	6 07	16	Lv. ....**Wilson**.....Ar.	8 13	1 07	10 25	
....	8 52	2 32	6 16	20	" ...Contentnea ⊙ "	8 05	1 00	10 16	
....	f8 58	f2 37	f5 22	23	" ...Black Creek⊙ "	f8 00	f12 54	f10 10	
....	†9 10	f2 50	f6 34	30	" .....Fremont..⊙ "	f7 46	f12 41	f9 58	
....	†9 16	f2 56	f6 40	33	" .....Pikeville..⊙ "	f7 40	f12 35	f9 52	
....	9 30	3 10	6 58	41	Ar. .**Goldsboro**.⊙ Lv.	†7 25	12 23	9 37	
....	P.M.	3 15	7 16	41	Lv. .**Goldsboro**.. Ar.	A.M.	12 10	9 32	
....	....	f3 32	f7 33	50	" .....Dudley...⊙ Lv.	.....	f11 49	f9 15	
....	....	f3 43	f7 44	55	" ..Mount Olive⊙ "	.....	f11 37	f9 05	
....	....	f3 50	f7 51	59	" .....Calypso..⊙ "	.....	f11 26	f8 58	
....	....	†3 56	f7 56	62	" .....Faison ...⊙ "	.....	f11 22	f8 52	
....	....	f4 03	f8 04	66	" .....Bowden...⊙ "	.....	f11 12	f8 44	
....	....	f4 12	f8 12	70	" ....**Warsaw**.⊙ "	.....	f11 02	f8 36	
....	....	f4 26	f8 26	77	" ...Magnolia..⊙ "	.....	f10 45	f8 22	
....	....	f4 36	f8 36	83	" ...Rose Hill..⊙ "	.....	f10 33	f8 13	
....	....	.....	f8 44	87	" ...Teachey..⊙ "	.....	f10 24	f8 05	
....	....	f4 48	f8 48	89	" .....Wallace ..⊙ "	.....	f10 19	f8 01	
....	....	f4 54	f8 53	92	" .....Willard...⊙ "	.....	f10 12	f7 55	
....	....	f5 00	f8 59	95	" .....Watha ...⊙ "	.....	f10 04	f7 49	
....	....	f5 14	f9 10	102	" ....Burgaw ..⊙ "	.....	f 9 48	f7 36	
....	....	15 23	f9 20	107	" .....Ashton.... "	.....	f 9 36	f7 26	
....	....	f5 30	f9 32	110	" ..Rocky Point⊙ "	.....	f 9 30	f7 20	
....	....	f5 40	f9 44	116	" .Castle Hayne⊙ "	.....	f 9 20	f7 10	
....	....	.....	.....	122	" .....**Gorden**.... "	.....	.....	.....	
55	**51**	5 54	9 59	123	" ..Union Depot..	**54**	9 06	6 56	**50**
P.M.	A.M.	6 00	10 05	124	Ar.**Wilmington**⊙ "	P.M.	*9 00	*6 50	A.M.
*3 45	*6 00	P.M.	A.M.	124	Lv. **Wilmington** Ar.	1 40	A.M.	P.M.	12 05
3 51	6 06	.....	.....	125	" ..Union Depot.. Lv.	1 34	.....	.....	11 59
....	....	.....	.....	126	" ......Hilton .... "	.....	.....	.....	
....	....	.....	.....	127	" .**Yadkin Jct** "	.....	.....	.....	
f4 00	f6 15	.....	.....	129	" .....Navassa .... "	f1 24	.....	.....	f11 49
f4 11	f6 26	.....	.....	135	" .....Malmo..... "	f1 10	.....	.....	f11 38
f4 25	f6 40	.....	.....	143	" ...Brinkley ..⊙ "	f12 57	.....	.....	f11 25
f4 44	f6 57	.....	.....	153	" .....Bolton ..... "	f12 40	.....	.....	†11 08
4 58	7 11	.....	.....	160	" Lake Waccamaw⊙ "	12 27	.....	.....	10 55
f5 07	f7 19	.....	.....	164	" ...Hallsboro.... "	f12 18	.....	.....	f10 48
5 21	7 29	.....	.....	170	" ...Whiteville.⊙ "	12 06	.....	.....	10 37
f5 35	f7 41	.....	.....	177	" .**Chadbourn**⊙ "	f11 53	.....	.....	f10 26
f5 48	f7 54	.....	.....	183	" ..Cerro Gordo⊙ "	f11 40	.....	.....	f10 13
f6 00	f8 06	.....	.....	189	" ...Fair Bluff..⊙ "	f11 27	.....	.....	f10 01
f6 18	f8 21	.....	.....	198	" .....Nichols...⊙ "	f11 06	.....	.....	f9 43
†6 32	f8 34	.....	.....	205	" ....Mullins...⊙ "	f10 52	.....	.....	f9 29
6 50	8 50	.....	.....	213	" .....Marion...⊙ "	10 35	.....	.....	9 12
7 10	9 05	.....	.....	221	" .....**Pee Dee**.⊙ "	10 18	.....	**82**	8 57
f7 20	f9 15	.....	.....	225	" ....Winona .... "	f10 08	.....	.....	f8 48
f7 27	f9 22	.....	.....	228	" ..Mars Bluff.⊙ "	f10 02	.....	P.M.	†8 42
‖7 40	9 35	.....	.....	234	Ar. ..**Florence**.⊙ "	‖9 50	.....	8 10	‖8 30
9 55	11 30	.....	.....	282	" ......**Lanes**..⊙ "	8 05	.....	6 59	6 05
11 40	1 20	.....	.....	336	Ar. **Charleston** ⊙ Lv.	*6 15	.....	*5 30	*4 15
P.M.	P.M.					A.M.		P.M.	P.M.

‖ Meals. ⊙ Telegraph Station. f Stops on signal. † Daily, except Sunday. * Daily.

This 1906 timetable—the year of the Warsaw wreck tragedy—shows Atlantic Coast Line service through this North Carolina town.

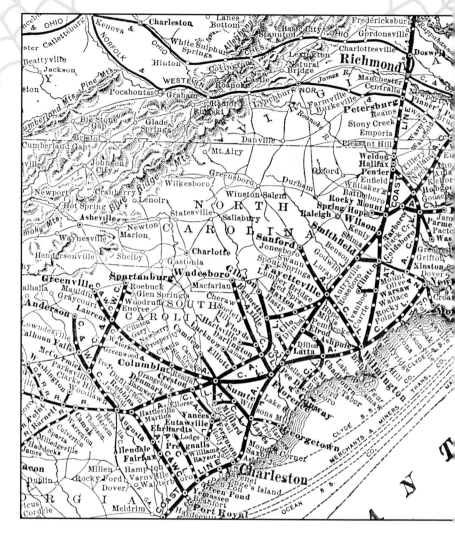

As the train approached, it hit the open switch at speed. The engine derailed and overturned. Burst steam pipes quickly scalded the trapped engineer and fireman to death. The baggage car also derailed and lurched halfway over. The baggage-master inside, his back broken by the impact, was trapped under tons of baggage. He screamed over and over, but when the passengers from the other cars finally reached him he was dead.

Soon after the accident, a family was walking home at night from the town's only hotel. Roads were bad, so they were walking

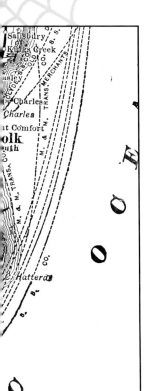

The Atlantic Coast Line in eastern North Carolina, circa 1906. Warsaw, which appears on the map, is said to be haunted by a ghost train; the hamlets of Maco, Mintz, and Vander, too small to be shown here, are all scenes of ghost light legends.

along the railroad tracks. They were on a trestle, a dangerous spot to be if a train comes by, when they heard a southbound extra whistle for Warsaw station. The piercing beam of a headlight stabbed towards them.

The family ran across the trestle to safety and stopped by the side of the tracks to let the train pass. The whistle sounded again and the headlight bore down upon them. And then, to their astonishment, the train simply disappeared!

Several nights later, the engineer of a northbound train whistled for Warsaw station. To his horror, he heard a southbound train, a train without rights to the track, whistle back,

ALCOHistoric Photos

Atlantic Coast Line Ten-Wheeler (4-6-0) No. 326, shown in a 1900 Richmond Locomotive Works builder's photo, is typical of turn-of-the-century ACL motive power. The accident that sparked the Warsaw ghost train legend is said to have happened in 1906.

The former Atlantic Coast Line main through Warsaw, North Carolina, now a CSX branch. It was here that citizens began seeing a phantom train after a fatal derailment in 1906.

and a headlight shone in his face. The engineer put the brakes into emergency and the train ground to a shuddering halt.

The trainmen back in the passenger cars knew something was wrong when they felt the sickening lurch of emergency brakes. They ran up the track to investigate, but nothing was there.

Apparently, the ghost of the wrecked train was appearing in Warsaw. Many people saw it back in the early years of the century, although it hasn't reappeared for a long time. Perhaps, as time passed, it just faded away.

"The Catsburg Ghost Train"

Catsburg Store, long a Durham, North Carolina landmark, is an old-fashioned general store catering to the hunters, fishermen and loafers of the neighborhood. Many years ago, a man was decapitated by a train at a road crossing near the Catsburg Store. Ever since, the Norfolk and Western track running by the store has been haunted.

Phil Petty, who frequents the Catsburg Store, says he's heard many a tale about the ghost.

"It's a headless horseman who was killed by a train," Petty says. "He comes riding up the tracks behind the store at midnight. We used to play at the ball field near the store and then watch for him on our way home. We always had to be home before twelve, though, so I never got to see the ghost."

Other folks say if you go to the road crossing near the store on a clear night and wait long enough, you'll see a headlight appear down the overgrown tracks. Off in the distance, you'll hear the huff of a steam engine and the clickety-clack of steel wheels on jointed rails. But the train, mysteriously travelling a track that hasn't been used since 1983, will never come.

Caroline Weaver

The Catsburg ghost train is said to roam this unused ex-Norfolk and Western branch line just north of Durham, North Carolina.

The headless ghost of Catsburg, North Carolina.

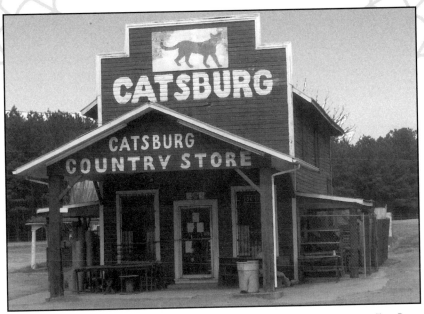

Patrons of the Catsburg Store, Durham, N.C., tell many a tale of haunted trains along the nearby Norfolk & Western track ever since a man was decapitated there by a train. A major segment of this former N&W branch from Lynchburg, Virginia has been out of service since 1983.

Ghost Train of Dalton, Georgia.

This ancient ghost story comes from an old "Railroad Magazine", and apparently caused a great deal of discussion among Western & Atlantic Railroad workers during 1881. The Western & Atlantic Railroad, scene of the famous locomotive chase between the "General" and the "Texas" during the Civil War, is now part of CSX.

A mysterious apparition was seen one night recently. The narrator was walking the track of the Western & Atlantic Railroad about two miles from Dalton when he discovered the headlight of a locomotive approaching around a curve. Strange to say, he heard no noise as the train came speedily on.

Presently he stepped from the track and waited for it to pass. No noise attended the engine's

Western & Atlantic No. 54, Acworth, was built by Baldwin in the year the ghost train of Dalton, Georgia appeared: 1881.

approach. As she came opposite, he noticed that the whole machinery had a ghostly, phantom-like appearance. At the throttle stood a pale, wild-eyed engineer, while a specter-like fireman was pulling the bell rope. But no sound came from the bell. All this he observed as the train rushed past him like a shadow!

It is interesting that this ghost train appeared along the route of the Great Locomotive Chase. Maybe the Western & Atlantic ghost train was a folklore echo—or a psychic echo—of that tragic, heroic, and emotional Civil War drama.

"The Ghost Train of Nineveh Junction"

Some years ago, but in the not too-distant past, a young man was driving the narrow, winding road leading from New York's State Route 7 up the hill to the Nineveh Hotel. The sky was deep purple/blue as the last rays of the fading spring twilight were disappearing in the western sky. Upon approaching the crossing of the Delaware & Hudson's Binghamton line, the red crossing lights started flashing their time-honored warning. The gentleman stopped his

Does the wraith of a steam-powered Delaware & Hudson train haunt Nineveh Junction? In this vintage photo, a train led by D&H No. 524 (a 4-6-0 Ten Wheeler built in 1904) passes a crossing shanty in the line's headquarters city of Albany, New York. The famous Delaware & Hudson Building is visible in the background.

automobile and consigned himself to wait for the approaching southbound train. Suddenly it caught his attention that the locomotive was not sounding its horn as is prescribed in all railroad rule books and, in fact, was proceeding towards the crossing at a very fast clip, but accompanied with no sound whatsoever. No squealing wheel flanges against the rail, no whistle or bell, no locomotive sound...nothing.

As if this wasn't startling enough, the locomotive was of the old-fashioned steam type, not a modern diesel. And, instead of the train being the typical freight, this was a passenger train; but no such train had run on the line since the early 1950s, over twenty years before. Through the windows, dimly lit from inside, could be seen the shadows of passengers sitting in their coach seats and eating in a dining car: nebulous shadows brought out by the pale amber lights and diffused by the speeding motion of the train on its silent, eerie journey.

As the apparition disappeared around the curve down the track and the crossing flashers stopped their red warning signal, the driver could see several people in front of the Nineveh Hotel nonchalantly passing the time as if nothing had happened. A check some time later revealed that the Delaware & Hudson Railway, although it did on occasion operate special steam-engine powered moves, had not at this period in time had any steam locomotives operating on their property, nor had they operated any type of passenger equipment through Nineveh Junction during the time in question. The ghost train will likely always remain a mystery.

Yazoo & Mississippi Valley Ghost Train

A young African-American brakeman was working a freight from Cleveland, Mississippi to Memphis, Tennessee in 1913. The train had orders to meet another train, No. 777, at Shelby, Mississippi.

The brakeman was riding three cars back from the engine. Suddenly, the train made an emergency stop and the engineer whistled out a flag to protect the front of the train.

The brakeman jumped off the freight car he was riding and ran ahead. He had his white lantern and, as he ran by the engine, the fireman handed him a red lantern.

California State Railroad Museum, Railway & Locomotive Historical Society Collection
Yazoo & Mississippi Valley mixed train, Shaw, Mississippi, pulled by locomotives #14 and #76. Shaw is just south of Cleveland and Shelby, Mississippi.

The brakeman ran a couple of hundred yards ahead to a tangent section of track. As he did, he could hear his train reverse and back away. The brakeman was left alone at his post for over two hours.

Finally, he heard his train slowly approaching. The brakeman stood in the middle of the track and signaled with the red lantern to show where he was.

The engine stopped and the brakeman climbed in. The crewmen in the cab were silent. The brakeman set his lanterns down and took a seat.

Finally, the conductor spoke. "What did you see while we was gone, Suggs?"

"Not a thing, sir, except for my own lanterns," the brakeman said.

"We seen a train, Suggs," the man said. "Three hundred yards ahead of us here. We thought we'd overlooked orders and met No.777 between stations. So we whistled out a flag and stopped. But then there wasn't no train."

He looked over at the engineer and the fireman and they nodded. "So we backed up to Cleveland and wired ahead to Shelby to be sure. No. 777 has been waiting there on a siding for us the whole time. There isn't any other train."

The three men sat silent while the young brakeman began to shake with fear. He started to think about standing there alone by himself for two hours —what if the ghost train had run by?

When the freight got to Shelby, No. 777 was still there, waiting for them on the siding. As word of the ghost train spread, several engineers told of seeing ghost lights between Cleveland and Shelby. This was the first time anyone had seen a phantom train. Old-timers said a train had wrecked along there around the turn of the century, killing the engineer and fireman. Was the wrecked train returning as a ghost?

The Ghost Train of Gaskins, Arkansas

The Missouri & North Arkansas was one of the most ill-fated of American railroads, rarely earning a profit and ceasing operations in 1946. It ran from Joplin, Missouri through the Ozark Mountains to Helena, Arkansas, a town on the Mississippi River. A ghost train that

appeared on the old M&NA in 1911 was described in "Railroad Magazine" many years ago. According to the magazine:

Phantom trains have long been subjects for the most exciting fiction, but it is seldom that a well-authenticated instance of such apparitions occurs. A story from Eureka Springs, Arkansas seems to fill the bill in this particular, however.

The engineer of a passenger train was about to slow up for the water tank at Gaskins, as was his custom, when he saw just ahead a caboose with the signal lights burning. He also saw the conductor come out of the cupola with his lantern and noted the burning fusee on the track.

He yelled to his fireman. The fireman glanced out of the window, saw the caboose, grasped the reverse lever, and helped his chief to throw it over; then both men dropped down to jump. But before they could go over, the caboose vanished and the only thing left was the charred fusee on the track.

Fireman Harrelson had such a fright that he refused to go out next morning; and although Engineer Dobbins went out under protest, he recommended Master Mechanic Dolan to have everything

This Missouri & North Arkansas Mikado, No. 19, built in 1910, was brand new when the phantom train made its mysterious stop at Gaskins, Arkansas.

in readiness, as there was sure to be a wreck somewhere.

But trains ran as usual, and if there was any object in the visit of the ghost train it has not been made clear yet. The account is supplemented by the statement that Agent Braswell, of Gaskins, also saw the phantom caboose and lights from his home.

The ghost train never reappeared and today the M&NA is no more. The stretch of track through Gaskins to Eureka Springs, Arkansas is still in service today, however, as part of the Eureka Springs & North Arkansas Railway, a tourist railroad.

The Ghost Train of the Arizona Desert

There are many stories of ghost trains chugging down America's tracks. But rare indeed must be stories of ghost trains that run where a real, iron and steel locomotive never has.

Southeastern Arizona, though, is said to be haunted by such a train. The story is that a prospector was lost on the alkali flats north of Arizona's Dragoon Mountains. He'd left Tombstone planning to prospect in Dos Cabezas, fifty miles northeast. Now his burro was dead and he was staggering across the flats in the white heat of day. The odds were that he'd die there before sundown and his bones would bleach in the hot Arizona sun.

He must be going crazy, he must, because far off in the distance he heard the clickety-clack of a train and the chug-chug of a steam locomotive.

That's when he remembered—the ghost train. Men—old miners, Mexicans—had told him about seeing the train on the flats where no train ever really ran. No one knew why it was there. It never stopped, just roared by and vanished in the desert sun.

Now, the prospector could hear a far-off whistle. He squinted his alkali-dusted eyes. Across the flats, shimmering with a mid-day mirage of blue water, he saw a black speck coming towards him, getting bigger and bigger.

Then, it was closing in on him. As it did, he could make out a headlight, a spark of light that looked strangely yellow in the remorseless white glare of the desert sun. Finally, he could make out the whole train —a black engine, blowing a cloud of smoke and steam, pulling two yellow coaches. The train was old-fashioned, like something the prospector remembered from Civil War days.

The train looked like it was going to run him down and, sure enough, it began tolling its bell as if to warn him of danger. The prospector tried to move but he couldn't. He realized with a shock that he was too far gone to move, a victim of sun stroke, unlikely to survive more than another hour or two of the fierce heat.

Just before it would have hit him, the train stopped. The prospector couldn't believe what happened next. As he passed out from the heat, strong hands seemed to lift him aboard the train. Someone stretched him out in the aisle of one of the passenger cars. The last thing he remembered was begging the people aboard the train for water.

Water was what woke him, water tricking over his face. He opened his eyes. A strange man wearing a sheriff's badge was standing over him holding a pitcher of water. "Man found you five miles out of town," the sheriff said. "You wouldn't a lasted another hour in that heat."

"Town, what town?" the prospector asked.

"Willcox, Arizona," the sheriff said. "What are you, loco?"

Last thing the prospector remembered, he had been twenty or

thirty miles from Willcox. He struggled up on his elbows.

"The train," he said.

The sheriff looked at him. "Ain't no train around here," he said.

The prospector eased himself back down. He thanked his lucky stars that the ghost train had decided to make its only stop ever—for him.

The Southern Pacific Railroad came through Arizona in 1880, running right through Willcox. It even put a branch into Tombstone. But Tombstone old-timers say that the ghost train still runs across the trackless alkali flats where no railroad was ever built.

Belleville, Texas's Phantom Train

During the night of January 10, 1960, a man on a business trip stopped for a train at a lonely grade crossing on Texas Highway 36 between Belleville and Sealy, Texas. At first, things seemed routine; but then the man noticed that the train, pulled by an ancient-looking locomotive, was emerging from a cloud of fog.

That's when the witness realized that there were no railroad crossing lights or signs at the site. The train, a long freight, passed slowly in front of his car, and the witness realized with a shock that it seemed to be lighted by something other than his car headlights.

After the train passed, the man looked around and realized that there was no railroad track at the point, not even a break in the pavement. He had seen another, inexplicable ghost like the one that runs through the Arizona desert: a phantom train that runs where no railroad ever did.

Ghost Train of Mayer, Arizona

Often confused with the ghost train of the Arizona desert is the tale of the Mayer, Arizona ghost train. The story is one of the oddest and most complicated of America's ghost train legends.

During 1893, the small mining town of Mayer, Arizona was shaken by the passage of a ore train rumbling through town on its way to a nearby smelter. Folks didn't think much about it until someone noticed the train had no engine: it was a runaway.

Nearby stations were warned by telegraph. A few hours later, though, the train rumbled back through town in the opposite direc-

The Mayer, Arizona railroad station.

tion. Mayer sat in a depression compared to the surrounding terrain, and it looked like the train was seesawing back and forth — running out of town in one direction until gravity stopped it, then reversing course and going back the other way.

The train soon came back through for a third pass at Mayer. Just when residents thought the train might roll on forever, a couple of old railroaders caught the train and braked it to a stop. The train halted on the tracks just outside of town. Stations up and down the line were notified, but no one could figure out where the train came from. After sitting in Mayer for days, the train disappeared one night.

The townspeople couldn't understand it. No one saw the train leave, no one heard a chuffing steam engine. Finally, an old miner came up with a far-fetched explanation. In 1871, he recalled, twenty-two miners escaped a flood in the Iron King mine by packing themselves onto a mine-train engine, No. 22. They uncoupled the locomotive and chugged out of the mine just as it filled with water.

So, the old miner said, twenty-two years ago number twenty-two took twenty-two men out of the mine without a train. Now, twenty-two years later, had old Number Twenty-two returned as a train without an engine? Unfortunately, no one had counted to see if the vanished train was twenty-two cars long.

Was the old miner right? Did the rescuing engine return as a ghost train twenty-two years later?

Ghost Train of Marshall Pass

The old narrow-gauge Denver & Rio Grande main line over Marshall Pass is gone now. Many years ago, it was the scene of one of America's most famous ghost train incidents.

Back when the Marshall Pass line was only a few years old, a passenger train was climbing to the twelve-thousand foot summit. The engineer got a signal on the cab gong to stop, and ground the train to a halt. Just as he stopped, he heard a whistle somewhere behind. Soon, the conductor came running up and demanded to know why the train was stopped. He hadn't given any signal, he said.

The engineer had started on his run feeling uneasy for no particular reason and this incident really jittered him. He had to meet train No. 19 and another was following him close, so he was in a dangerous situation by the time he got his train moving. He heard a whistle again, looked back, and saw with horror that a train was speeding behind him, going much faster than he was. A collision seemed inevitable.

The now-frightened engineer pulled the throttle wide open and his engine plunged forward like a frightened rabbit. His train rocketed through clogged snowsheds and across rough track, in danger

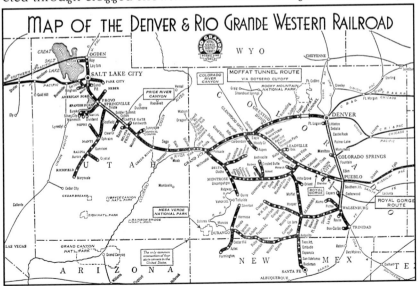

This 1940 system map shows the Denver & Rio Grande Western's now-abandoned narrow-gauge line over Marshall Pass.

of plunging off the rails at any minute. The engineer kept the throttle open, though, because the train behind was catching up.

The fireman and most of the passengers saw the train following. A wild rumor swept through the coaches that the second train was being run by a crazy engineer, determined to collide with their train.

The engineer reached the summit of Marshall Pass, and muttered a prayer under his breath. He looked back —and the following train was still there. It was close enough now that he could make out details: the engine's drivers were big, bigger than the ones on his engine, and a man stood on top of one of the cars, waving frantically.

A sharp curve approached, and the engineer looked back again. The following train was just a couple of hundred yards away. Then the engineer saw something that chilled him through and through. As his train reached the middle of the curve, he could see the engineer of the following train clearly. The man was leaning out of his cab, laughing! His face was white like the face of a corpse.

Snow began falling, and still the chase was on. The engineer reached a bridge with a low speed limit, but he didn't dare slow down. He rocketed across the bridge, and still the second train followed him, seeming to gain on his train foot by foot.

Now, the engineer could see the switch lamp marking the siding where he had orders to meet No. 19. The engineer's blood ran cold when he saw No. 19 was not waiting in the siding —now he might be rammed from ahead as well as behind. Just past the switch, he saw a red light waving across the track —the railroader's signal for danger ahead.

Denver Public Library;
Western History Department,
photo by Charles Redmon
A Denver & Rio Grande passenger train on Marshall Pass. A scene like this must have inspired the famous Marshall Pass ghost train legend.

Without even thinking about it, the engineer reversed the engine and threw on the brakes. He began to pray again, and expected any minute to feel the jolt as the pursuing train rammed his, killing who knows how many passengers back in the coaches.

He waited for a second and, feeling no crash, looked back. He saw the pursuing train, yards away. Suddenly, just before the pursuing train crashed into his, the track seemed to spread, the engine rolled off the side of the mountain, and the entire train rolled into the canyon. The engineer listened for the sound of the crash at the bottom but all he could hear was the whistle of the wind.

The engineer had more surprises in store that night. Looking at the track ahead again, he saw that the caution signal had also vanished. It wasn't No. 19 after all—the opposing train must still be ahead of him.

The engineer got his train into the next siding before No. 19 passed by. He finished his run to Green River, and here's perhaps the strangest part of the tale. As he got ready to leave the engine, he

The message left by the ghost train of Marshall Pass.

found a message traced in the frost on his cab window. "A frate train was recked as yu saw," it said. "Now that yu saw it yu will never make another run. The enjine was not under control and four sexshun men wor killed. If yu ever run on this road again yu will be recked."

This mystery was too much for the engineer. He quit the Denver & Rio Grande that day and got a job with the Union Pacific.

Workmen went out the next day, but found no train wrecked in the canyon. The phantom train of Marshall Pass was never seen again.

Kansas Pacific Ghost Train

Edwardsville, Kansas was located twelve miles west of Kansas City on the Kansas Pacific Railroad. One day in 1878, an Edwardsville farmer, Mr. J. F. Timmons, was in his house when a Kansas Pacific section gang ran in, frightened for their lives. They told a weird story.

The section gang was working on the K. P. track running across the Timmons farm when they saw a storm blow up. They put their handcar on the track and started full speed for Edwardsville.

They hadn't gone very far when they all saw what they thought was a locomotive. It was coming around the curve east of Edwardsville at a high rate of speed.

The men managed to get their handcar off the track in time, and then stood waiting for the engine to pass them. What they saw, though, made them run for Timmons's house.

The thing was not a locomotive, but a cloud of dense smoke. The center of the cloud gave off occasional flashes resembling a headlight. It ran down the track three-fourths of a mile from where the section men first saw it, then turned off the track. It circled a pile of cordwood at the side of the track once, then went off in a south-westerly direction through a dense wood. That's when the men ran.

What came down the Kansas Pacific track that July day in Edwardsville?

North Shore Railroad locomotive No. 18 with train at Fairfax, California c. 1904-1905, with engineer Billy Richie (left) and fireman Bob Rutherford (right).

Retribution: A Mystery Story of White's Hill

This unique story of ghostly revenge comes from the Northwestern Pacific (a northern California railroad) publication, "Headlight", dated 1928. It is perhaps the most literary, well-developed American railroad ghost story:

> Our party consisted of a group of good fellows, mostly professional men, who had been invited by Dr. Black for several days of quail hunting in the Marin Hills.
>
> Had the worthy surgeon known beforehand that the elements were going to be as rough as they were, or had he known what the consequences of that weekend, of what was his intention to be one of pleasure for all concerned, really meant, it is certain he never would at that particular time, have planned the trip.
>
> Our hunting ground was to have been in and

around the canyons and gullies on the eastern slope of White's Hill, in Marin county.

The Doctor explained, he had through a deal with the owner of the land, secured the hunting privileges, which carried with them, the right to stop with the Portuguese family, Gonzales by name, who leased the ranch for dairying purposes.

Mrs. Gonzales was a well spoken little woman, well educated and of a mental caliber far above the average women of her nationality and she was always glad to have and entertain Dr. Black and his friends, and the Doctor was likewise proud to have his friends with him on these trips, as Mrs. Gonzales set an exceptionally fine table, being a past mistress in the culinary art.

We arrived at the ranch on a Friday afternoon and as the quail season opens in December in California, the weather at that time of year is always uncertain. On this particular evening, large black clouds were driving from the southeast, a sure sign of rain and storm in this section, and one of our genial comrades remarked that it was the 13th of the month, Friday afternoon, and it appeared that our hunting trip was probably "jinxed."

We all joked at his pessimistic view of the situation and were soon comfortably quartered within the spacious ranch house and, as had been predicted by the Doctor, all of us were soon enjoying one of the best meals of which any of us had ever partaken.

Under the influence of the excellent food, which had been washed down by some of California's finest vintage, stories were told and the wit and repartee was highly enjoyable. So much so, in fact, that none of us was aware of the storm which had grown to furious proportions whilst we were regaling ourselves at the table, and probably would then have paid no attention to the weather, if a sudden gust of cold air had not almost extinguished the lamps, which at that time served as the only means of illumination on the ranch.

The gust of air was caused by the entrance of a neighbor, and the flare of the lamps caused a momentary pause in our festivities. Dr. Black in his usual good natured manner, requested Mrs. Gonzales to bring the neighbor in, intimating that he was probably wet and cold and in need of warmth and stimulant and, accordingly, Bill Springer was introduced to the assembled guests.

He explained he was a caretaker of an adjoining estate and was wont to visit the Gonzales family, and apologized for his seeming intrusion on the particular evening, stating, had he known the hunting party was there, he would not have come over. His little speech of apology, clearly and well put, indicated he was a man of some education. By way of conversation he asked Mrs. Gonzales if a recent guest of the ranch, a French artist, by the name of Pierre Godeaux, who had come up to make pictures of the beautiful Marin Hills, was still there.

Mrs. Gonzales informed him the artist had left very hurriedly the Sunday previously and explained she thought he was somewhat mentally unbalanced. When asked for a further explanation she produced a copy of the county paper in which was a news story of a French artist who declared that while walking one stormy night over the Gonzales ranch he was startled by hearing the whistle of a train, apparently on the old abandoned right-of-way of the old North Shore Railroad over White's Hill, and he had further declared that not only had he heard the afore mentioned whistle but had also actually seen the train. The article ended with the intimation that the artist was probably suffering from some nervous ailment or might possibly be demented.

Bill Springer listened to the reading of the item with more than passing interest and it was noticed, not only by the Doctor but by others of the party, that he had become exceptionally pale and a perceptible shudder shook his stalwart frame.

"Here Springer," said the Doctor, "take this," and he proffered a glass of brandy. "Your getting wet on your way over here evidently did you no good and might result harmfully."

As Springer slowly drained the glass, a blinding flash of lightening occurred, followed by a terrific crash of thunder, which reverberated in stunning echoes from the surrounding hills. Each of the Doctor's guests looked wide-eyed at the other and the Doctor, seeing that something should be said, quoted from Bobby Burns' Tam O'Shanter:

"The wind blew as 'twad blawn its last;

The rattling shower rose on the blast;

The speedy gleams the darkness swallow'd:

Loud, deep and lang the thunder bellow'd:

That night, a child could understand,

The Devil had business on his hand".

Springer by this time was rapidly pacing the floor and as the Doctor finished his short recitation, the applause which started, died suddenly when the party noticed that the afore mentioned paleness which had been noticed on Bill's face had developed into a distinct pallor. Several of the guests jumped to their feet and forced Springer into a chair before the fire and after he had downed a hot toddy made by the Doctor, he said—

"Pierre Godeaux is not insane! I also have seen that train, not once, but several times, and it only appears on stormy nights such as this."

Upon hearing this announcement, the entire group stared at Springer, and he again commenced to pace the floor.

The Doctor assumed his professional manner and, forcing Springer back in his chair, he said —

"See here, Springer, how could it be possible for

a train to be on this old right-of-way? There are no rails, no ties. The tunnels are caved in and only the remains of the trestles are left. The old road was abandoned in December, 1904, some twenty-three years back from this particular Friday night."

Bill listened and then, more like talking to himself than to the guests, remarked:

"Yes, that is right —it was in 1904 that the new tunnel was completed at which time the old five miles of road between Roy's Station and Maillairds, through two tunnels, across several high trestles and over the top of White's Hill was abandoned.

"I was told the original road was a hard one and it was necessary to have wood stations at frequent intervals between the foot of the hill and the summit. These stations were kept supplied by men employed for the purpose and they lived in a little colony which was located not far from here, just up the canyon.

"In this colony there also lived one of the engineers. Mahoney was his name and a finer Irishman never lived in Marin County. He was a widower with one daughter, who was a beautiful girl —"

At this moment Spring was seen to tremble violently and another drink was offered to him, but he waved it aside. "I'm all right now", he said.

"Well, Mahoney thought the world of his daughter, who, since her mother passed away, was the light of his life, administering to him as only a dutiful daughter can, and theirs was a happy household.

"And then came the tragedy —the same old story. A youth working in the wood gang —misplaced confidence and love —a ruined girl and the subsequent death of both her and her child in a San Francisco maternity hospital —an outraged father, who swore by all the Saints in Heaven, that he would some day get the guilty one, if he had to return from his grave to do so —and gentlemen —I believe," said Springer, "that the ghostly train seen by both Artist Godeaux and myself is piloted by Mahoney, looking for a chance to run down his daughter's unfaithful lover. You know, gentlemen, they say a criminal always returns to the scene of his crime, and Mahoney probably knew that too. By George! It's almost Midnight! The storm has somewhat abated and I had better be on my way."

The party looked at one another in amazement and Bill, seizing his hat and overcoat, stole away in the blackness. As the door closed behind him the storm again broke out in renewed fury and some ten minutes later, a flash of lightning, a crash of thunder, and the distinct shriek of a locomotive was heard by the assembled guests. Almost at the same moment, and hardly before the echoing thunder had subsided, a wild agonizing scream was heard by those in Dr. Black's party. Someone grabbed a lighted lantern that Gonzales had just placed on the kitchen table, after returning from her barn, and the whole party scrambled up the hill toward the quarter from which the scream had come. The doctor was the first to reach the old abandoned right-of-way and, with the aid of the rays of the lantern discerned what was left of Bill Springer.

One leg and one hand were cut off completely. As the doctor reached the mangled body and knelt beside it, Springer faintly murmured, "Mahoney got me at last."

Tightly clasped in his remaining hand was a piece of iron such as is used on the end of a passenger car, by travelers, to assist themselves in getting on and off, and stamped on the metal were the letters--N.S.R.R. Co.

On the following Monday twelve men, sitting as a coroner's jury in San Rafael, in the matter of the passing of one William Springer, after listening to the testimony of Dr. Black and his friends, brought in a verdict of "Death from cause or causes unknown".

White's Hill, in suburban Marin County near San Francisco, was the scene of Bill Springer's mysterious death.

The Phantom Locomotive, Number 110

One of the most spectacular train wrecks to occur near Alderson, West Virginia took place at Mohler's Curve about a mile below town at 1 o'clock in the morning, October 4, 1881, when engine Number 110 met engine Number 112 head-on. Both were pulling freights. Number 110 had a light train and was moving at about thirty-five miles per hour while Number 112 had a long train and was going about twenty miles per hour. The two approached unawares until they were upon each other because of the sharp curve at Mohler. When the train crews realized their plight, it was too late, but the engineer and fireman on the eastbound (Number 112) train jumped and saved themselves. The engineer and fireman of the westbound train both met death in the ensuing cataclysm of fire and steam. On the westbound, the brakeman, Lee Hill, son of

Chesapeake & Ohio No. 110—the phantom locomotive—in about 1890.

Spencer Hill of Alderson, was severely injured and eventually lost both legs, and every man on both train crews was injured to some degree. The impact was so terrific that both locomotives were completely destroyed and cars were piled up to a height of fifty feet and spread over several hundred yards of the right-of-way. Some of the trainmen were thrown through the air fifty feet by the jolt of impact only to get up practically unharmed. Doctors Barksdale and Spicer of Alderson attended to the dead and wounded and a large group of men from town came out to help extricate Lee Hill from under a box car where he was pinned. To get to him it was necessary to move a stack of 500 cross ties which were piled on the right-of-way; between these and the car he was trapped. As the rescuers struggled to free him he alternately prayed and cursed until he was free. By morning the wrecker from Hinton arrived with a crew and cleared the tracks. The hulks of the engines were taken back to Hinton and most of the cars broken up and burned, as indeed some had already been reduced to matchwood. The wreck was blamed on the night operator in the tower at Alderson who failed to hold the westbound train until the eastbound had passed.

A most unusual story is connected with this wreck. It was often told by Mr. J. H. Hoover of Alderson. It seems that he was head brakeman on the eastbound freight, pulled by Number 112, and was sitting atop one of the cars well back in the train. "It was a beautiful moonlit night and I could watch the scenery flow by. As we went up the long straight stretch above Riffe's Crossing I looked across the bottom and there stood a locomotive. Out there where there were no tracks and where no engine could be, it stood, clearly and plainly visible. The headlight was burning and the figures on the side were plain —'110'." Upon seeing this phantom locomotive, Mr. Hoover made his way to the engine and mentioned it to the engineer and fireman. He thought it was a warning.

Presently he saw the gleam of an approaching headlight on the rails ahead as they ran into Mohler's Curve. And then he jumped. "I rolled down the embankment like a bear and then heard the awful smashing and grinding as the two trains smashed into each other. Presently I was able to walk up to the place and there were the two engines reared into the air just like two dogs standing on hind legs fighting." He felt he already knew the number of the westbound engine, and sure, when he looked, it was Number 110. "Then I quit railroading."

Mr. Hoover's story can be considered a dream or just a fantasy made up to amuse or frighten, but he was not a man to do such things. He was a learned man and not given to superstitious feelings. He saw that phantom locomotive that night and the experience made him quit railroading for good. It is certainly one of the most interesting stories ever told about any wreck on the C. & O. (This information was supplied by Mr. J. B. Swope of Kimberly, W. Va.)

The Chesapeake & Ohio station in Alderson, West Virginia.

Ghost of the White Train

One of the most famous passenger trains in American history was the "White Train," the Boston-New York train of the New York & New England Railway. The train, whose formal name was the "New England Limited," gained fame because it was painted entirely white.

The train began running in 1884 and was painted white as a publicity stunt in 1891. It was thereafter known as the "White Train," but the public soon gave it a nickname: the "Ghost Train." The train was likened to a ghost due to its eerie appearance at night.

The train only ran in its white livery for four years. It was then replaced with another, faster train, the "Air Line Limited." Even though the "Ghost Train" vanished about one hundred years ago, it made such an impression that rail fans still recognize the name today.

The "Ghost Train" apparently

made another impression —an impression on the spirit world. It has been sighted in New Haven, Connecticut a number of times since the turn of the century. Close witnesses even report they've been able to see wide-eyed figures tearing at the coach windows from the inside as the train rushed by. Today, much of the old New York & New England is abandoned, although portions do survive near New Haven as part of Conrail.

History is silent as to why the "Ghost Train" reappears.

California State Railroad Museum, Railway & Locomotive Historical Society Collection

New York & New England No. 183 with the "White Train," also known as the "Ghost Train." Does it still run today?

Pittsfield, Massachusetts
Ghost Train

Another New England ghost train haunted the Bridge Lunch Diner in Pittsfield, Massachusetts in February and March, 1958. Workers and customers at the diner were often startled away from their coffee, flapjacks, hamburgers, and order pads by a old-timey passenger train made up of a steam locomotive, a baggage car and five coaches passing by on the tracks fronting the place. Calls to the railroad revealed that no such train was running at the time.

Pittsfield, once a junction between New York Central subsidiary Boston & Albany and the New York, New Haven and Hartford, is still an important point on Conrail's Boston-to-Albany main.

Phantom Locomotive of Stevens Point

Stevens Point, Wisconsin is said to be haunted by a phantom locomotive. Although never seen, the old steam engine is heard chugging

Collection of Dr. Art Peterson
The Stevens Point, Wisconsin Soo Line railroad station.

across the landscape. Witnesses claim that the engine always sounds like it's just around the bend, but that it never comes into view.

The town, located on the Wisconsin Central and the Green Bay & Western, is also said to be haunted by a phantom engineer. A figure, said to be the ghost of an engineer, has been seen close to a bridge on the line haunted by the phantom locomotive. According to local folklore, a train wreck at the bridge killed the engineer, who now haunts the scene of his death.

If local legend ever recognized a connection between the phantom locomotive and the ghostly engineer, it has been lost in the mists of time.

This photo depicts the aftermath of the Bostian's Bridge tragedy. A witness fifty years later described a ghostly reenactment of the same horrifying scene.

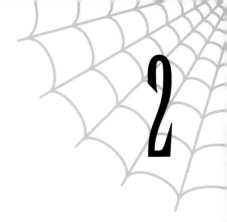

Wreck Re-enactments

*I*f there's any truth to the theory that hauntings are caused by a sudden release of some type of psychic energy, then ghost wreck reenactments are the easiest railroad ghosts to explain. As an event that suddenly sends a group of unprepared people to their deaths, a train wreck is fertile ground for the creation of ghosts.

It's also a fertile ground for the creation of folklore. Most wrecks happen in rural areas, where they are the biggest news event in years. They often remain the most memorable happening in a community's history.

Look at the Statesville wreck, for example. The train wreck at Bostian's Bridge in 1891 was one of the most costly, in terms of human lives, that ever happened in the South. It was a big news item in sleepy Statesville, North Carolina, and undoubtedly people began to tell stories about it soon afterward. That probably explains the genesis of the Statesville ghost legend.

The Statesville ghost train is also interesting in that it is said to appear only on the exact anniversary of the tragedy. Most of the other ghost wrecks described below aren't so exacting.

Ghost train legends do seem to have a certain pattern, however: a person alone at night hears a train and thinks it

is real. Then, the train wrecks and the person rushes forward to look at the tragedy, which vanishes. With some modifications, this is the American ghost train legend as it occurs across the country.

The Statesville Ghost Train

During the early morning hours of August 27, 1891, a passenger train left Salisbury, North Carolina for Asheville. The train never made it any farther than Bostian's Bridge, a sixty-foot-high, stone-and-brick-arch bridge over Third Creek. The 1858 vintage structure, which is used to this day, is near Statesville, North Carolina—the

Bostian's Bridge, near Statesville, North Carolina, as it appears today. The scene of at least one real and one spectral disaster, the bridge is located on Norfolk Southern's main line between Salisbury and Asheville, North Carolina.

next important stop after Salisbury on the line to Asheville.

At about 3 a.m., the ill-fated train derailed and plunged off Bostian's Bridge, falling sixty feet into the creek below. Twenty-two people died from the shock of the fall or from drowning in the waters of the creek. It was the worst wreck in North Carolina's history. Since that time, the Salisbury-Asheville line has become part of the Southern Railway System, now Norfolk Southern.

Our story now goes forward in time fifty years, to the early morning hours of August 27, 1941. A woman, stranded along the road that paralleled the Southern Railway near Statesville, was wait-

An artist's conception of the moment of disaster at Bostian's Bridge, near Statesville, North Carolina, on August 27, 1891.

ing for her husband, who had gone for help. They had had a flat tire. She heard a train whistle in the distance and a headlight appeared down the tracks.

As the train approached her, it began to cross a high bridge. Suddenly, the engine derailed and the train plunged off the bridge into a creek below. The horrible sounds of the wreck were soon replaced by the groans and cries of wounded people. The woman ran toward the wreck and looked into the creek bed. The sight was horrendous: the engine, tender, and passenger cars were a twisted mass of wreckage that was quickly being flooded by the waters of the creek.

Just then, she heard a car pull up behind her. She ran towards it, screaming that a terrible wreck had just happened. Her husband was in the car with a stranger, who owned a nearby country store. The men went to look at the ravine, but there was nothing there.

Apparently the train had been a ghost train, reenacting the wreck of 1891. Since then, Statesville youths have frequented the Bostian's Bridge area on night outings to look for the ghost, sometimes conducting informal seances there. On the hundredth anniversary of the wreck, August 27, 1991, newspaper stories about the haunting led hundreds of people to the bridge. Onlookers were parked all along the rural road that runs by the area waiting for the ghost train, while vendors sold shirts and drinks. While some ghost-hunters claim they did see or hear a ghost, most—including the author—agree it didn't appear. This impromptu anniversary gathering seems destined to become local folklore in its own right.

The Ghost Wreck of Zoar Valley

New York's Zoar Valley, near Cattaraugus, is said to be a haunted place, haunted by a murderer's curse. It is also said to be haunted by a ghost train.

A railroad, now abandoned, ran across Zoar Valley, connecting two towns separated by the rift. The railroad crossed the deepest part of the valley with a trestle. Every evening at ten o'clock a train roared across the bridge, making the ground tremble so much that folks living in cabins above the valley could feel it.

One dark, foggy night, the train approached the trestle at ten o'clock—right on time. Too late, the engineer saw that the trestle was out. Instead of the usual rumble, that night folks heard a horrible crash of iron on iron as the entire train tumbled into Zoar Valley. People could also hear the screams and groans of the frightened, the wounded, and the dying.

Today, most of the cabins that once perched above the valley are gone, as are the trestle and the train. But, if you go to the valley at ten p.m. on a dark, foggy night, you'll hear the train crash and the passengers scream.

The Phantom Wreck of Rowlesburg

In April of a year in the early 1900's, an eastbound, morning Baltimore & Ohio train was going downgrade into a valley near Rowlesburg, West Virginia. The train jumped the track and plunged down a two-hundred foot embankment.

It was a terrible wreck. Seven passengers were killed outright as they slept and many others were injured, some dying later. The cause of the wreck was never determined.

A few years after the wreck, two brothers were walking home at night and passed the scene of the accident. They heard a train whistle in the distance. The brothers knew that no train was due, so they stopped to see if it was a wreck train or some other unscheduled movement.

When the train came into view, they were amazed to see that it was an unscheduled passenger train. Suddenly, the train jumped the tracks and fell down the embankment. The wreck was eerie: the men could see the engine boiler explode and saw the passenger cars burst into flame, but the crash didn't make a sound!

Even so, the men decided to go for help. As they ran away, they looked back at the wreck scene. To their amazement, the burning train had disappeared. They ran over to the track and looked down the embankment —there was nothing there.

Did the ghost of the Rowlesburg wreck return?

McDonough, Georgia Ghost Train

According to local legend, a train approaching McDonough, Georgia in 1919 wrecked with such devastating force that all of the passengers and crew aboard were killed. Since then, the train and its doomed occupants have tried to reach McDonough safely. As the ghost train approaches the station, its whistle blows, the engines roar, and smoke belches into the air. People who hear the sounds always pause and look for a train, but the phantom rattler never reaches the station.

McDonough is located on the former Southern Railway line (now Norfolk Southern) from Atlanta through Macon to Brunswick, Georgia. It was once the site of a junction with a now-abandoned Southern Railway branch from McDonough to Griffin, Georgia.

The phantom wreck of Rowlesburg.

The ex-Baltimore & Ohio main line through Terra Alta, West Virginia as it appears today.

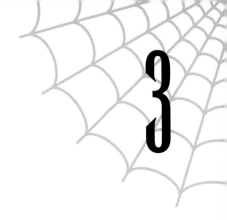

Headless Ghosts
and Ghost Lights

Ghosts along the tracks take many guises. The most common ones are headless ghosts and phantom lights. After you pass these categories, the rest are a ghostly miscellany of misty phantoms, ghostly music and more.

One of the most common railroad ghost stories in American folklore transcends the headless ghost/ghost light categories. It is found in many locations throughout the country, always with the same basic features. For the sake of description, let's call this story the "headless railroader." As the story comes to us from states as different as New York and Georgia, the headless railroader ghost is that of someone killed along the railroad tracks, usually a railroad employee. In most cases, the ghost was beheaded by a train and returns as a headless phantom, usually to look for its head. It may appear without a light, with a light or simply as a light. As you'll see below, a large number of the ghosts along America's tracks fit into this basic story cycle.

This story cycle seems to offer a lot of possibilities for further study. Why, for example, is it so popular? Where did it originate and how did it spread? Do all of these stories derive from a common ancestor, or did they evolve coincidentally?

Headless Ghosts

Headless ghosts are common in American folklore, and railroad folklore is no exception. The reason for our national obsession with headless phantoms is unknown. Perhaps this macabre way of dying captured the imaginations of those who told these tales.

It is interesting to note that one of our best-known railroad folk songs, "In The Pines" or "The Longest Train," tells of the death of a young girl whose "head was caught in the driver wheel, Her body I never could find." This song shows that the drama created by a headless victim transcends the ghost folklore genre.

Whatever the reason, many of the ghosts reported along railroad tracks in America are headless. What's more, many of them carry lights, usually ghost lanterns, linking them to the ghost light stories we'll look at later in the chapter.

The Headless Brakeman

Up in New York, there was a boomer brakeman named Tolley who was deadheading home in a caboose one day. The night was dark, stormy, and icy. One of Tolley's friends, who was the regular brakeman on the run, was out on the car tops.

As the train rounded a dangerous curve, it hit a washout and the engine and the first ten or twelve cars derailed. Tolley, who was unhurt, walked up the train to see about his friend. The unfortunate brakeman was lying under one of the cars, decapitated.

The shock of seeing his friend killed made Tolley settle down. He took a fireman's job on the same railroad, and eventually became an engineer. He always tried to avoid the run that his friend had been killed on, but was eventually assigned to it.

It was take it or lose his job, so he took it. One rainy, cold night, he was approaching the bad curve where his friend had been killed. He saw a red light up ahead, and threw the brakes into emergency. The fireman went up the track to look, but couldn't see anything.

Tolley was sure he had seen a warning light, so he walked up to take a look for himself. The light reappeared right away, and Tolley walked toward it. As he got closer, he could see that the light was an old-fashioned, red, railroad lantern. As it swung from side to side in a warning signal, or "washout," the lantern seemed to illuminate a man clad in the blue overalls worn by old-time brakemen.

Tolley was excited now, and began running towards the brakeman, yelling, "What's the matter? What's the matter?" When he got close enough to see the figure clearly, he stopped suddenly and shook with terror: the brakeman had no head!

Suddenly, there was nothing there. Sure that this was a warning from his old friend, Tolley walked around the curve. And Tolley was right—there was a washout at the same place where the fatal wreck had happened so many years ago.

After the wrecking crew cleared the tracks and Tolley brought his train home, he handed in his resignation.

The Headless Ghost at Free Springs Bridge

Just southeast of Sullivan, Indiana is a place called Free Springs. A railroad passes through parallel to a small stream; a gravel road crosses the railroad tracks and then over the stream on a bridge.

Several ghost legends have grown up about the Free Springs Bridge, two of which focus on the railroad nearby. According to local legend, a headless body was found under the Free Springs Bridge many years ago. No one could identify the body, and most folks assumed the dead man was a tramp who had been murdered and dumped from a passing freight train. The head was never found, and the body was buried without it.

Ever since the body was found, strange noises and sightings of headless ghosts have been reported at the bridge. The bridge is a favorite haunt of local teenagers, who go there at night to try and spot the ghost.

A related legend is that of the ghost with a lantern that haunts the bridge. According to this story, a trainman fell off a caboose and was beheaded by the wheels of his train. Today, if you go to the Free Springs Bridge and park on it, you can look down the railroad track and see the headless ghost. He walks the track at night, waving a lantern, looking for his head.

The Headless Trainman of Fairmont

Just before World War I, the Baltimore & Ohio had a unique way of signalling engineers when to slow for the station at Fairmont, West

A ghost in search of his head has been a long-time resident of Fairmont, West Virginia. It was near this station site that an unfortunate B&O trainman was decapitated. Local residents believe his spirit returns, lantern in hand, looking for his head.

Virginia. A chain hung over the track, it would hit the train, and the noise would tell the engineer it was time to slow down.

One evening, just at dusk, a trainman was riding the car tops. He wasn't looking ahead and he didn't notice the chain. It hit him over the shoulders, wrapped around his neck and snapped his head off. The unfortunate man's body and head then fell to the ground. No one saw the accident, the train kept going, and the man's remains weren't found until later on.

After that, the railroad removed the chain. But they couldn't remove the ghost of the trainman. People walking the track at dusk would see a lantern ahead at about the spot where the chain had hung. As they got closer to the lantern, they could see it was held by a headless man. If they kept walking towards the ghost, it would cross the track and disappear.

Folks in Fairmont believe the phantom is the ghost of the decapitated trainman, looking for his head.

The Body Under the Train

Years ago, the section of Baltimore & Ohio track east from Terra Alta, West Virginia was overseen by a section foreman named Mr. Wilburn. Three of the sectionmen—Joe, Bob, and Dick—roomed in Mr. Wilburn's house.

Bob and Dick were bachelors, and every payday they headed to Terra Alta for a night on the town. One payday, Bob was assigned to take the night shift walking the track. He wanted to go to Terra Alta and Joe, who was married, needed the money, so they switched off.

After a night of drunken gambling, Dick was thrown in jail for disturbing the peace. Bob had to walk home down the track without a lantern.

On his way home, Bob had to walk through a deep cut. He couldn't see anything as he tramped through the excavation without a light. The cold wind funneled through the deep man-made ravine, making eerie noises. As he listened, Bob remembered the evil reputation of the place, and shuddered as he recalled some of the stores he'd heard about it. He started walking faster.

About halfway through the cut, Bob stepped on something soft. He thought it was an animal that had been killed by a train, and reached down to throw it off the track. His groping fingers felt locks of hair, eye holes, a nose—it was a human head.

Bob ran for the Wilburn house, screaming. It took an hour for Mr. Wilburn and his wife to calm him down enough to tell them what had happened. After hearing Bob's story, Mr. Wilburn and a neighbor walked back down the track and found Joe's body. He had been hit by a train and beheaded.

Several days later, Bob quit his job with the B&O. He told Mr. Wilburn that Joe was haunting him, and that he kept seeing Joe's headless body under a coach of the night train. Mr. Wilburn kept telling Bob that there were no ghosts, but Bob quit and left Terra Alta for good.

Ghost Lights

Ghostly lights—usually headlights or lanterns—are common along America's railroads. They often occur in conjunction with something else: a headless railroader looking for his head by lantern-light, perhaps, or a ghost train preceded by an eerie headlight in the distance. Sometimes, though, they occur by themselves, and those are the stories I've gathered here.

In fact, America's most famous railroad ghost, the Maco Light, is nothing more than a hovering glow said to be the light of a long-dead conductor's lantern. This phantom was seen by thousands during its long career of appearances in North Carolina's coastal plain, and it has been mentioned in a number of books.

Conditions in coastal North Carolina and Virginia must be right for whatever phenomenon, natural or otherwise, that causes ghost lights along railroad tracks. In addition to the Maco Light, Mintz and Vander in coastal North Carolina and Cohoke and Suffolk in eastern Virginia have their own ghostly lights.

The phenomenon also extends to rural New Jersey, to a place called Long Valley that is haunted by a similar light. An investigation of the Long Valley light led to the theory that railroad ghost lights are caused by an electrical interaction between the rails and rock formations underlying the tracks. Since the lights often seem to date back to the construction days of the railroads they appear along, and since they tend to disappear when the rails are taken up, this theory seems to warrant further investigation. Perhaps more research would mean that America's many railroad ghost lights could finally be explained.

The Maco Light

Maco Station, North Carolina is a tiny point on what was once one of the Atlantic Coast Line's many tracks radiating from Wilmington, North Carolina. The hamlet is located fourteen miles west of Wilmington in the flat piney barrens of North Carolina's coastal plain.

The long history of the Maco Light begins back in the days of wood-burning steam locomotives and link and pin couplers. Joe Baldwin was a conductor on the line just after the Civil War, and

ATLANTIC COAST LINE

FLORIDA
CUBA
SOUTH

ATLANTIC COAST LINE

INFORMATION AND SCHEDULES

"CONSULT THE PURPLE FOLDER"

FLORIDA'S FAMOUS TRAINS
"NEW YORK & FLORIDA SPECIAL"
"FLORIDA & WEST INDIAN LIMITED"

OFFICES

NEW YORK
B'way cor. 30th St.

BOSTON
298 Washington St.

PH LADELPHIA
1019 Chestnut Street

BALTIMORE
Corner Light and
German Streets

WASHINGTON, D. C.
1419 New York Av., N.W.

made many runs out of Wilmington.

One day in 1867, Joe was riding on the last car of a passenger train when the car's coupling link broke near Maco Station. Joe rushed to the back of the car and put on the brakes. The car began to slow to a stop.

Unfortunately, another train had been running close behind Joe's train. Joe saw its approaching headlight, realized the danger, and began signaling wildly with his lantern. With the bravery typical of railroad men, he stuck to his post, waving his lantern, even as the other train bore down on him.

In those days, before the advent of air brakes, the outcome was almost inevitable: the other train could not stop in time, and it plowed right into the coach ahead. Joe was decapitated by the tremendous impact. His body was crushed into the coach, and his head, which flew into the nearby swamp, was never found. Joe's lantern was torn from his grasp. It flew off to the side of

The Atlantic Coast Line's routes in eastern North Carolina were haunted by ghost lights at Maco, Mintz, and Vander.

Tony Reevy

Thousands have visited this lonely spot in Maco, North Carolina looking for the Maco Light. The light stopped appearing when the railroad was abandoned.

the tracks, its light describing a bright arc. It landed, miraculously, upright and still burning.

Soon after the accident, a light began appearing at Maco Station. Folks thereabouts said it was old Joe looking for his head. It appeared so often that trainmen on the division had to use two lanterns to signal at Maco Station rather than one so crews wouldn't be misled by Joe's ghostly light. In 1873, two lights began appearing, and people said Joe's head was also looking for his body. Following the 1886 earthquake, the two lights disappeared for a time. After a little while one of the lights reappeared, while the second hasn't been seen again.

In 1889, Grover Cleveland's presidential special stopped at Maco Station for fuel and water. He saw trainmen using two lanterns there, asked about it, and was told the whole story. In more recent times, Atlantic Coast Line trains have actually stopped for the Maco Light, believing it to be a signal or another train.

During the '40s and '50s, going to see the Maco Light became a popular teenage summertime outing in the Carolinas. Viewers who saw the light always reported the same thing: the light flared up way down the track, crept toward the observer, then speeded up and began swinging side-to-side. Finally, the light stopped abruptly, hovered for a minute, retreated back to where it started from, and vanished. The light always appeared three feet above the left rail, facing east. It was sometimes so distinct that you could see the metal guards of a railroad hand lantern. The light didn't appear every night: it seemed to appear randomly, according to old Joe's whims.

In the late sixties, the old Atlantic Coast Line, which was headquartered in Wilmington for many years, merged with former rival Seaboard Air Line to form Seaboard Coast Line. This line has since merged with the Chessie System to form CSX. The Seaboard Coast Line and CSX have followed a policy of ruthlessly abandoning excess trackage. All but one of the lines running into Wilmington have been severed in recent years—including the line through Maco Station, which was abandoned in 1977. Local folks say Joe hasn't appeared since the tracks were taken up. Perhaps he's angry or depressed about the abandonment, or maybe he's just confused. Maybe he'll even come back some day.

The abandoned Atlantic Coast Line Wilmington-to-Sanford branch is still a readily-visible swath through the woods in Mintz, North Carolina. It was here that the Mintz ghost light appeared until the tracks were taken up in recent years.

The Phantom Stationmaster

Closely related to the Maco Light story is the eastern North Carolina legend of the phantom stationmaster. According to this legend, an old stationmaster was working at a small depot just outside of Wilmington, North Carolina. One stormy night, he got an order to stop an oncoming train. The old man put on his raincoat and hat, lighted his red lantern, and stepped out on the platform.

The weather was terrible, with rain coming down in torrents. The wind was so strong that it nearly knocked the stationmaster down. From even a few feet away, all you could see was the dull, red glow of the old man's lantern.

Hearing the train whistle its approach, the old man stepped on the tracks and held up his red light. The train's headlight appeared in the storm, but the engine's exhaust didn't slacken. The stationmaster, amazed that the engineer wasn't slowing for his signal, began to wave his lantern frantically across the tracks: the standard railroad danger signal, or "washout."

The engineer, peering into the storm, never saw the old man. The old stationmaster stuck to his post; the train ran him down, passed over his body and continued on.

Although the accident happened in the early 1900's, locals say that a dull red glow still appears at the old railroad station site on nights when there's a full moon. If you stand right by the tracks, you can't see the light; you have to get at least twenty feet away or it won't appear.

The Mintz Ghost Light

Like Maco, Mintz, North Carolina is a lonely spot along an abandoned ex-Atlantic Coast Line branch. The hamlet is located between the tiny towns of Roseboro and Garland, North Carolina. A light appeared along the railroad grade here for many years and, according to local folklore, it was the ghost of a railroad employee.

According to local residents, the railroader was employed as a track watchman, "clocking" the trains as they ran through the lonely coastal swamps. One night he was startled by a train as it high-balled along the tracks. He fell into the path of the train and was beheaded by the remorseless iron horse. His head and body were never found. A more dramatic version of the story insists that, after

Tony Reevy

The Mintz Baptist Church, just east of the abandoned stretch of track where the Mintz ghost light once appeared regularly, mystifying thousands of witnesses over the years.

the watchman was beheaded, his decapitated body groped for his lantern, picked it up, and vanished.

After the watchman's death, a light began to appear at Mintz — a glow that hovered over the railroad tracks, bounced and disappeared. Local folks claimed that the light was the dead track watchman's ghostly lantern.

According to local residents, the light was a nightly occurrence in Mintz during the early 1960's. Carloads of people from surrounding towns would drive to the tiny crossroads community to witness the light. Some local folks even drove to the spot every week just to see it. It didn't scare people because it had always been there and they had grown up with it.

Like the Maco Light, the Mintz ghost light stopped appearing when the tracks through town were taken up in 1980. People in the area have stopped talking about the ghost, and its story seems to be fading out of local folklore.

WILMINGTON AND SANFORD.

53	Mls	STATIONS.	52	
*9 10A.M.	0	Lv...**Wilmington**.⊙ Ar.	8 00P.M.	
9 20 "	2	" ....Yadkin Junction .Lv.	7 47 "	
f9 35 "	9	" ......Richards...... "	f7 32 "	
f9 49 "	16	" .....Montague... "	f7 19 "	
f9 55 "	19	" ......Currie......⊙ "	f7 13 "	
f10 08 "	25	" .....Atkinson...... "	f7 00 "	
f10 23 "	32	" ......Ivanhoe...⊙ "	f6 46 "	
f10 32 "	36	" ......Kerr........ "	f6 37 "	
f10 42 "	41	" ....Tomahawk.... "	f6 28 "	
f10 55 "	47	" .....Garland..... "	f6 16 "	
f11 04 "	52	" ...Parkersburg.⊙ "	f6 06 "	
f11 24 "	61	" .....Roseboro....⊙ "	f5 48 "	
f11 43 "	69	" .....Autryville...⊙ "	f5 32 "	
f11 50 "	72	" ......Stedman...... "	f5 25 "	
f11 59A.M.	76	" ......Vander....... "	f5 17 "	
12 20P.M.	83	Ar.. **Fayetteville**.⊙ Lv.	5 00 "	
12 35 "	83	Lv.. **Fayetteville**... Ar.	4 55 "	
f1 02 "	95	" ....Manchester.. Lv.	f4 30 "	
f1 17 "	102	" .. Spout Springs.⊙ "	f4 16 "	
f1 33 "	109	" ...Rock Branch.... "	f4 00 "	
f1 37 "	111	" ......Swann...... "	3 57 "	
1 50 "	117	" ....Bonesburg..⊙ "		
1 55P.M.	119	Ar......**Sanford**....⊙ Lv.	*3 49P.M.	

The ex-Atlantic Coast Line route from Wilmington to Sanford, North Carolina was haunted by ghost lights at Mintz (between Roseboro and Parkersburg) and Vander. The line, originally built by the Cape Fear & Yadkin Valley, is now largely abandoned.

The Vander Ghost Light

Like Mintz, Vander, North Carolina is located on the ex-Atlantic Coast Line branch from Wilmington to Sanford, an almost entirely abandoned line that was once part of the Cape Fear & Yadkin Valley Railway. Unlike Mintz, Vander is still served by the railroad, now CSX. The town, which is a few miles east of Fayetteville, is located on a vestigial stub of the old Wilmington-to-Sanford line.

A light appears on the old railroad tracks in Vander, a phantom that looks very similar to the Mintz and Maco Lights. In this case, however, many local residents don't have a traditional explanation for the light. Witnesses say the glow, reportedly the size of a human head, bounces above the tracks and disappears. It can be seen from over two hundred feet away.

Some in the area claim that the light is the ghost of a switchman killed when shifting cars at the siding in Vander. Others claim that the light is the ghost of the driver of a mule wagon. The wagoner, residents say, was decapitated in a grade crossing accident at Vander and returns from his grave to look for his head.

Vander residents wonder if the light might be caused by swamp

CAPE FEAR & YADKIN VALLEY R. R. COMPANY.

Cond. Schedule—In effect May 7 1893.

S. Bound Daily. No 1	MAIN LINE.	N. Bound Daily. NO. 2
11 00 p m	Ar........Wilmington,......Lv	5 00 a m
7 46 p m	Lv......Fayetteville,........Ar	8 02 a m
7 20 p m	Ar.....Fayetteville,.........Lv	8 12 a m
6 00 p m	Lv..........Sanford,.........Lv	9 30 a m
4 13 p m	Lv...........Climax,.........Lv	11 44 a m
3 45 p m	Lv........Greensboro.........Ar	12 15 p m
3 40 p m	Ar........Greensboro.........Lv	12 25 p m
2 57 p m	Lv.......Stokesdale,......Lv	1 22 p m
2 30 p m	Lv..N.& W.J'ct—W.Cove..Ar	1 55 p m
1 5? p m	Ar..N & W. P'ct—W.Cove,Lv	2 33 p m
1 22 p m	Lv.......Rural Hall,......Lv	3 02 p m
12 00 m	Lv..........Mt. Airy............Ar	4 25 p m

Daily. No 3		Daily. No 4
10 15 p m	Ar........Bennettsville,.......Lv	5 40 a m
9 20 p m	Lv...........Maxton,...........Lv	6 30 a m
8 49 p m	Lv.........Red Springs,......Lv	7 02 a m
8 05 p m	Lv.........Hope Mills,.........Lv	7 43 a m
7 47 p m	Lv.......Fayetteville.......Ar	8 02 a m

No. 15 MIXED Daily Ex Sunday.		No 16 Mixed Daily Ex Sunday
5 55 p m	Ar..........Ramseur,..........Lv	6 25 a m
4 15 p m	Lv..........Climax,........Lv	8 15 a m
3 00 p m	Lv........Greensboro..........Ar	9 00 a m

No. 15 MIXED Daily Ex Sunday		No 16 Mixed Daily ex. Sunday
2 35 p m	Ar........Greensboro,........Lv	9 20 a m
1 25 p m	Lv.........Stokesdale, ... Lv	10 35 a m
12 25 p m	Lv..........Madison........Ar	11 25 p m

All Trains daily except Sunday.

Train No 2 connects at Sanford with Seaboard Air Line for Raleigh, Norfolk and all points North and East, and at Walnut Cove with the Norfolk and Western R R for Winston-Salem, Roanoke and all points North and west of Roanoke.

Train No. 1 connects at Walnut Cove with Norfolk & Western R. R. for Winston-Salem, Roanoke and all points North and West of Roanoke, and at Sanford with Seaboard Air Line for Monroe, Charlotte, Athens, Atlanta and all points South and South-West.

Pullman Palace Sleeping Car on Seaboard Air Line trains North and South from Sanford and on Norfolk & Western trains North and West from Roanoke.

Passengers from Wilmington, Fayetteville, Maxton, Bennettsville and all points South of Sanford will arrive at Raleigh at 11 15 A. M., and have five hours in Raleigh and reach home the same day.

Ample time is given passengers for breakfast at Sanford, dinner at Walnut Cove, and supper at Fayetteville.

J. W. FRY,   W. E. KYLE,
   Gen'l Mang'r.   Gen'l Freight Agt.

ALCO Historic Photos

Above: Cape Fear & Yadkin Valley No. 13, a 4-6-0 built in 1886, is an example of the engines that hauled CF&YV trains through Mintz and Vander, North Carolina before the railroad's acquisition by Southern and Atlantic Coast Line.

Tony Reevy

Right: The rarely-used CSX tracks through Vander, North Carolina are a haunting setting for the appearances of the Vander ghost light.

Above: The Cape Fear & Yadkin Valley Railroad ran from Wilmington to Mt. Airy, North Carolina, as shown in this rare 1893 timetable. The railroad was later divided between the Atlantic Coast Line (Wilmington - Sanford) and the Southern Railway System (Sanford - Mt. Airy).

gas, static electricity or ball lightning. Still, none of these causes seem to adequately explain a light that can appear regularly, whether or not a train happens to be approaching.

The Cohoke Ghost Light

Cohoke, Virginia is a tiny hamlet located on the ex-Southern Railway (now Norfolk Southern) branch from Richmond to West Point, Virginia.

According to railroad historian Robert Reisweber, a ghostly light appears along the Norfolk Southern tracks at Cohoke. Reisweber states that local legend identifies the light as the ghost of a conductor killed by beheading in an accident at Cohoke. A check of railroad records, however, failed to find any mention of employee fatalities there. Some locals, Reisweber reports, say the light is the conductor's lantern, while others say it's too bright to be a lantern and believe it's the headlight of the conductor's train.

A persistent legend says that the light is the ghost of a Confederate hospital train that disappeared on the line during 1864. Reisweber disputes this explanation, noting that the rail line through Cohoke was held by the Union Army during the 1864 siege of Richmond.

Smithsonian Institution Photo No. 61281-Y

Southern Railway No. 942, a 4-6-0 built in 1893, at the West Point, Virginia Southern Railway station in 1936. West Point is the terminus of the ex-Southern branch running through Cohoke, Virginia.

Proponents of the hospital train story say two lights are seen. One is the headlight of the vanished hospital train, while the other is a lantern carried by the ghost of a Confederate soldier. The soldier appears well in front of the ghost headlight and floats ten feet or so above the tracks. Only the soldier's head, shoulders and arms may be seen, and his features are blurred.

One witness reports that as the large, brilliant light folks thereabouts think is a ghost headlight passed a parked car, the occupants flicked on their headlights. As the area around the ghostly glow was illuminated by the car lights, the witness saw the outline of a train.

One of the most amazing things about the light is the number of people who have seen it. Over the last hundred years, thousands have reportedly witnessed the light, which seems to appear and disappear at random. The light is said to be very bright, too bright to be swamp gas, and it is said to appear all year round. It does usually appear on cloudy nights, often during a storm or a rain shower.

The light has been described as a big, bright, round ball and as a gaseous glow. It appears several hundred yards down the tracks from witnesses, then moves towards onlookers, becoming brighter as it nears them. Witnesses are often frightened away as the light approaches. The light disappears if assailed by foolhardy folks who shoot at it or try to run it down with their cars as it passes the grade crossing in Cohoke. No one has successfully photographed the light.

Other witnesses have reported experiencing a strange feeling before the light appears: a strong impression that someone else is

BRANCH LINES—(Richmond Division)—WEST POINT AND RICHMOND.

No. 75 Ex. Sun.	Mixed No. 9 Mon Wed and Fri	No. 15 Daily	Miles	Eastern Time		No. 74 Ex. Sun.	Mixed No. 10 Mon Wed and Fri	No. 16 Daily
				Lv	Ar			
1 30PM	10 00AM	8 00AM	0	WEST POINT	Va.	9 00AM	4 15PM	6 00PM
1 46 "	f10 10 "	f 8 08 "	4	Romancoke ..	"	f 8 35 "	f 4 04 "	②547 "
1 59 "	f10 17 "	f 8 16 "	8	Sweet Hall ...	"	8 16 "	f 3 55 "	f 5 38 "
f	f10 22 "	f 8 20 "	10	Cohoke.......	"	f	f 3 49 "	......
2 18 "	f10 29 "	8 27 "	13	Lester Manor..	"	7 50 "	3 41 "	5 26 "
2 27 "	10 33 "	8 31 "	15	White House..	"	7 35 "	3 25 "	......
2 42 "	10 43 "	8 41 "	19	Tunstall......	"	7 20 "	3 12 "	5 11 "
3 00 "	f10 54 "	f 8 50 "	23	Quinton......	"	7 02 •	f 3 60 •	f 5 02 "
3 11 "	f10 58 "	①855 "	25	Dispatch.....	"	f 6 50 •	f 2 51 •	......
3 26 "	f11 05 "	f 901 "	28	Meadow......	"	6 43 "	f 2 45 •	f 4.53 "
3 46 "	f11 13 "	①909 "	31	Fair Oaks....	"	f 6 30 "	f 2 36 "	②446 "
4 25PM	11 35AM	9 30AM	39	Ar RICHMOND	Lv	6 00AM	2 15PM	4 30PM

①Stops on signal on Sundays, Mondays, Tuesdays, Thursdays and Saturdays.
②Stops on signal on Tuesdays, Thursdays and Saturdays.
Euclid Heights is flag stop for Nos. 9, 10, 15, 16.

This 1913 Southern Railway System timetable shows a flag stop at Cohoke, Virginia, home of the Cohoke ghost light.

there. The light then materializes, sometimes pacing witnesses' cars as they drive the section of road in Cohoke parallel to the railroad tracks.

Like the Maco and Mintz ghost lights, the Cohoke light has attracted a great deal of attention from area residents. In fact, ghost viewers were once so numerous that they came by the carload, blocking the road in Cohoke (Virginia 630/632). People have also been known to fire at the light with shotguns, endangering less violent thrill-seekers. So many people frequented the area to watch for the ghost light that the county finally passed an ordinance prohibiting loitering in the area after dark. This may be one of the few times that a ghost has created government regulation!

The Suffolk Ghost Light

Suffolk, Virginia, is a Tidewater-area community located on the very edge of the Great Dismal Swamp. The town was once an important rail center, and is still criss-crossed by railroad tracks.

Townsfolk report a ghost light, very much like the Cohoke light, that appears on a bleak stretch of railroad tracks at the fringe of the Great Dismal Swamp near Jackson Road. The road is a country lane close to the North Carolina border.

People who've seen the light report a glow that suddenly illuminates the area and then is gone. Others report a light that bobs up and down as it moves along the track; a light that looks like the glow from an old-fashioned kerosene lantern.

The light, which can be quite bright, has been seen moving up and down along the tracks for as long as an hour at a time. It is usually seen in late summer or early fall.

Locals have several versions of why the light appears. All say the light is the ghost of a brakeman killed at the spot, but they differ from there. One version says the brakeman, who had a very sick child, left home in a terrible storm to flag down a train to send for medical help. The engineer didn't see the brakeman in time and ran him down, decapitating him. Others say the brakeman was trying to flag a train to warn its crew of a tree downed across the tracks by a storm when he was hit and killed.

Finally, many people say that, like Joe Baldwin, the brakeman was killed by decapitation in a train wreck. Folks say the brakeman is wandering the tracks through eternity, still looking for his head.

The Hookerman

Long Valley, New Jersey, located on an abandoned Central Railroad of New Jersey railroad grade, is the scene of another phantom light said to be the ghost of a dead railroader. The light appears on a level stretch of right-of-way located between Naughtwright Road and Seven Bridges Road, a very isolated rural spot.

The story goes back to the immediate post-Civil War era, when the Central Railroad of New Jersey line through Long Valley was new. It was the pioneer era of railroading, when operations went on without air brakes and with the old-fashioned link and pin coupler. According to local folklore, a brakeman switching cars on the fly was crushed between two boxcars. The unfortunate brakey lost his arm, lingered on for several weeks and finally died.

After the accident, a mysterious light appeared along the CRRNJ right-of-way at frequent intervals. The light started appearing before there were electric lights or car headlights, so they can't explain the phenomenon. A scientific investigation of the light theorized it was caused by an unexplained interaction between the CRRNJ rails and a bed of quartz underlying the track. Nothing was proved, however, and no one could ever come up with a definite explanation for the phantom light.

Locals have a more colorful explanation of the phantom. They say it is caused by a ghost that some folks have seen, the ghost of the

Railroad Museum of Pennsylvania

Central Railroad of New Jersey No. 277, a Baldwin 4-6-0 built in 1872, is typical of the nineteenth century motive power that may have steamed past the Hookerman's wraith.

A period view of the Central Railroad of New Jersey station in Long Valley, New Jersey--home of the Hookerman.

crushed brakeman. The brakey, known locally as the Hookerman, appears as a one-armed man holding a railroad lantern walking down the tracks at the scene of the long-ago accident. Folks say that the light people see is the gleam of his lantern as the Hookerman looks for his long-lost arm.

A slightly different version of the tale explains the name, Hookerman. This version claims that the brakeman got drunk or fell asleep, pitched off his train, and got his hand cut off by a railroad car. His hand was replaced by a hook. Later, after the ex-brakey passed away, his ghost started re-visiting the area, looking for his hand. As the phantom searches in the dark, he holds a lantern in his hook.

The tracks through Long Valley were removed about ten years ago and, like the Maco Light and the Mintz ghost light, the Hookerman's light apparently vanished with the rails.

The Headless Engineer's Light

About a mile from Chapel Hill, Tennessee, the old Louisville & Nashville Railroad crossed a gravel road. According to local legend, a L&N engineer was killed there in the 1890's. He was leaning too far

The Hookerman.

from the cab window and, when the train went into a sharp curve, he was pitched out. He was decapitated by his own train.

Even in modern times, the engineer has returned looking for his head. After a night freight passes at 9:30 or so, a light appears and sways back and forth over the track. Locals say the light is the ghost of the headless engineer, looking for his head.

Other witnesses claim that the ball of light travels in a straight line along the tracks, and is capable of passing through the bodies of watchers without harming them. The Chapel Hill light has even passed through a car stalled on the tracks.

The Senath Ghost Light

This story comes from the state of Missouri. It originates in Senath, a town located on the old St. Louis-San Francisco (Frisco) Railway. According to John L. Yarbro:

> Southeast Missouri is typical Mississippi River delta country; low and flat. The only high ground you will ever see there will be a levee, an Indian mound or a train track bed. Several years ago, a new interstate and bridge opened up Southeast Missouri to Tennessee. Before the bridge, there was the ferry. With the bridge came the opportunity for new friendships to form and I met a few people who became really good friends. In the course of one of our conversations, ghost stories came up and they offered to take me out to see the Senath Light.
>
> Way out in the middle of nowhere in Southeast Missouri is a community called Senath (pronounced zenath) that has a most peculiar and famous ghost. It seems this fella was working for the railroad and somehow or another there was a terrible accident where he was beheaded. Every night, just after midnight, you can drive to a point out in the country where the train bed crosses in front of you and see this light, which comes from around a bend, crosses slowly in front of you, turns around and retraces its path. It goes on like this for hours until just before daylight when it disappears. The light is an amber/reddish glow reminiscent of old time lanterns. Anyway the light represents that beheaded man looking for his head. Now I've seen the light from a car, but I didn't get out for a closer look. Over the years I've met a lot of people from the surrounding area who have seen the light. No explanation has ever been given other than the one above.

Collection of Dr. Art Peterson

The Frisco station in Senath, Missouri. Senath is the site of the Senath ghost light.

The Crossett, Arkansas Ghost Light

The railroad track through Crossett, Arkansas is on a fill about three feet above the elevation of the surrounding countryside. At a road crossing, humped across the elevated tracks, the Crossett ghost light appears.

According to local legend, a train stopped at this point on a hot summer night and a brakeman walked back to check the train. He leaned in to check a coupling just as the locomotive lurched momentarily and slack ran along the cars.

The engineer saw the brakeman's lantern disappear after the sudden jolt. Fearing the worst, he ran back along the train and found the unfortunate trainman beheaded under the wheels of one of the cars. The body was put in a boxcar to make its long, last ride home. Some say the head was never found; others say that it was placed in a different car as it was carried back.

The trainman evidently misses his head because he keeps coming back to look for it. People say that they see his lantern moving along the tracks about three feet above the ground. The light appears as a dim, yellow ball about a foot in diameter. People in the

Crossett area claim that the light has been seen for over half a century, and that it still appears today. Like the ghost light of Chapel Hill, Tennessee, the Crossett light is said to sometimes pass through the bodies of watchers standing on the tracks without harming them.

The Concord Ghost Light

One of the oldest ghost stories in this book is the Concord Ghost Light. On December 4, 1888, a young brakeman named Alexander Campbell was working on a Richmond & Danville freight train running through Concord, North Carolina. The train was switching at the Concord depot when Campbell, a brakeman, slipped climbing a ladder between the cars.

According to period newspaper accounts, "he fell to the track and the wheels passed over his body, breaking his legs and arm, and so otherwise injured him that he died in a few hours." The railroad called down a local doctor and a doctor from Charlotte, but medical aid proved to be useless.

Collection of Emily J. Patterson

Alexander Campbell was a young brakeman killed in an accident on the Richmond & Danville at Concord, North Carolina. He became a celebrated legend in the area during the late nineteenth century when many witnesses claimed to have seen a disembodied lantern at the scene of the accident, now on a Norfolk Southern main line.

Soon thereafter, Richmond and Danville workers began to see a ghostly light at the Concord depot. The December 14, 1888 "Concord Times" noted that, "just before it (a train) reached the spot where the brakeman was killed the other day, the engineer saw a lantern waving in front of him. He stopped the train when the light went out. He then passed on and looking back saw the light again waving. The train hands refused to go back to examine, and they of course believe it was the ghost of the dead brakeman."

The Concord ghost light became well known, and was described in other publi-

Amtrak's "Carolinian" passes the site of the old Southern Railway station at Concord, North Carolina in 1993, enroute from Charlotte on Norfolk Southern's busy main line. The switch where Alexander Campbell's ghost reportedly appeared was probably located just beyond the grade crossing visible in the photograph.

cations as well. The light was said to appear nightly at the switch where Campbell was killed and give the same danger signal. Another account of the light's appearance notes that a young telegraph operator, Sapp, was sent back to the switch where the light appeared. According to the article, "Upon his near approach the signal suddenly disappeared. The moon was shining brightly and there was no place to conceal any one."

The article could not explain what caused the light if it wasn't a ghost. "...those who are not superstitious cannot account for the affair. The switch is near the railroad bridge, and all the country is clear and dry about it. Sapp was within a few feet of the signal when it disappeared. Mr. Ryder (the superintendent) and many others saw the danger signal and the lights working."

Alexander Campbell's ghost light seems to be forgotten now, but it was news during the late years of the nineteenth century. Did Campbell return to the scene of his gruesome death? Why did his ghost light fade away while others seem to have survived to the present day?

Johnny Marsden's Light

Like the Concord ghost light, the reappearance of Johnny Marsden's lantern is directly linked to a railroad tragedy. One morning in the fall of 1907, a local freight was making the run between Argenta and Brinkley, Arkansas on the old Rock Island line. Johnny Marsden, a brakeman working the run, was walking over the car tops towards the head of the train as it ran along. Marsden slipped, fell and was killed as the wheels of the local ran over him.

Several days later, the head-end brakeman who had been working the run with Marsden was flagging at a place called Lonoke. He had just stopped a passenger train and was talking with its crew. Suddenly, a light appeared down the tracks, moving towards the men from the village of Kerr, Arkansas. Both of the trains were to meet an opposing train in Kerr.

The brakeman assumed the light was a lantern held by a brakeman walking towards him. He walked towards the light, intending to meet the other brakeman halfway. When the brakey got within about a quarter-mile of the lantern-light, however, he saw it turn off the tracks, move down the hillside and vanish.

The brakeman was frightened by the light's strange behavior. He investigated the spot where the light had disappeared, but didn't find another brakeman or a lantern. He returned to his former spot and found that all of the passenger train's crew had also seen the lantern vanish. None of the men could account for the light's strange disappearance.

When the two trains finally met the opposing train in Kerr, the brakeman asked if anyone on that train had walked towards him with a lantern. It turned out that no one had.

The Rock Island station in Lonoke, Arkansas. Johnny Marsden's light appeared here in 1907.

The mystery of the vanishing lantern was never solved. Some of the train crews believed that the light was Johnny Marsden's ghost, holding his lantern as he tried to get to his train —one more time.

Red Light for Danger

Many years ago, a fireman was killed in a terrible derailment on the Southern Pacific line through Monument Point in Nevada. For many years afterwards, train crews were stopped at the site by a swinging red light —the standard railroad danger signal. Crews would look for the light and for whoever had signaled them, but never found anything.

The Big Thicket Ghost Light

Big Thicket is a wild area, dense with undergrowth, located in Texas near the small town of Saratoga. The wilderness is located between the Trinity and Neches Rivers. Big Thicket's only open spaces are roads, railroad rights-of-ways and a few clearings. The ghost town of Bragg, a former trackside community, is located in Big Thicket.

During the Civil War, the densely overgrown area was a hide-out for draft-dodgers, Union sympathizers and bandits. Confederates conducted war-time "burn-outs" in the area to flush out those avoiding service in the Confederate army. During one such burn-out in the village of Kaiser, the house of a "jayhawker" (Union sympathizer) was burned and the man, his clothes afire, ran into Big Thicket. He burned to death there, his flaming body catching some of the clinging overgrowth on fire.

Local hunters say that the man still haunts Big Thicket, appearing as a ball of flame. The Big Thicket ghost warrants a mention here because he developed the habit of following the Santa Fe Railway tracks through Big Thicket when the railroad built across the area later on.

Others say that, like many ghost lights along America's railroads, the Big Thicket light is the ghost of a brakeman, Jake Murphy. Murphy, who lived in the now-deserted town of Bragg, slipped on a rainy, muddy night and fell under his train. He was decapitated and his body was cut to pieces; his head was never found. Local folks say that the light is Murphy looking for his head.

Others say that the light is the ghost of four Mexican section hands who were murdered and robbed by their foreman. The bodies were found by a railroad worker who had befriended one of the murdered men. The foreman was tried and found guilty of murder. Apparently human justice hasn't satisfied the dead section hands, who still wander the tracks looking for their hard-earned, stolen pay.

Still another local legend says that the ghost is the spirit of a Bragg hunter who disappeared in the swamps and bogs of Big Thicket. Despite a two-day search by volunteers, no trace of the missing hunter was ever found. People claim that he still roams the area trying to find his way back to his family in Bragg.

The Santa Fe line through the Big Thicket area was abandoned very early on, in 1934. After that, the ghost light followed the abandoned railroad right-of-way. The right-of-way is now a sandy lane known as Bragg Road.

The main road through Big Thicket was paved in 1952. Since then, more people drive through the area and the light has been seen frequently. It often appears on dark nights as a ghostly glow moving slowly through the tangled undergrowth.

Many who have seen it describe it as a light that appears to come from a kerosene lantern swinging back and forth as someone carries it along to light their way. It varies from a dim yellow to a bright white to a deep red.

Glowing Eyes on the Track

One day in 1927, an eighteen-year-old boy was walking home from a movie show in Pikeville, Kentucky, a town located on the old Chesapeake & Ohio Railway in the eastern part of the state. It was about midnight.

There had been a big storm and the water was high. The boy walked into a cut near Cedar Creek and saw them—eyes. Two eyes, a few inches apart—he could see them glowing in the darkness but they vanished whenever the lightning flashed.

The boy got off the tracks and threw two big rocks at the eyes and they seemed to go right through the thing. The boy couldn't figure out what the thing was —it wasn't a train; in fact, it didn't make any noise at all. The thing kept coming nearer, going straight down the tracks. After it passed the frightened boy, he couldn't see the eyes any more.

What walked down the C&O tracks that midnight back in 1927?

"The fight at the water tank" (top) and "The death of 'Railroad Bill'" (bottom). From J. B. Harlan's article in the L &N Employes' Magazine, *May, 1927.*

Other Ghosts Along the Tracks

Ghosts haunt railroad rights-of-way just like they do houses or graveyards. Railroad tracks have been the scene of violent death for many an unfortunate worker, trespasser or passenger, so it is easy to understand why they are the scene of many a ghost legend.

This group of ghosts from along the tracks is a miscellany, ranging from a train robber who could turn himself into a dog or fox all the way to the ghost of an Irish laborer, entombed inside one of the supports of an abandoned railroad bridge.

If any theme ties these legends together, it is one of return: victims returning to the scene of a tragedy, workers returning to their work site, a native American warrior returning to his homeland, Railroad Bill returning to the scenes of his crimes, an old man returning to the happy home of his last years.

Among these legends, one of the most interesting categories is the ghost tramp. To this observer, the fascinating thing about this type of tale is its rarity. Although thousands of tramps were killed on America's railroads down through the years, they almost never return after death; ghosts along the tracks are usually railroad employees and are almost never hobos. Perhaps this is because the tales were originally told by railroad employees, who generally bore an animosity for tramps.

Perhaps the ghost tramp is rare for a different reason: because the tramp traveled alone and died unknown in a strange place. Transience, whether represented by a moving train car or a roaming tramp, seems to be the major enemy of ghost legends. They need roots and time to develop.

Railroad Bill

Railroad Bill, Railroad Bill,
He never worked and he never will
I'm gonna ride old Railroad Bill.
Railroad Bill he was a mighty mean man
He shot the midnight lantern out the brakeman's hand
I'm gonna ride old Railroad Bill.

Railroad Bill," American folk song.

Railroad Bill's home is the Alabama woods along the old Louisville and Nashville Railroad. Railroad Bill is a man, a black man, a backwoods Robin Hood who steals food from country stores and railroad cars and gives it to the poor. Many poor old widows in rural Alabama have woken up to find a pile of food on the front porch, left in the night by Railroad Bill.

Many, too, are the stories told about Railroad Bill by the people of the Alabama piney woods. Like the time the sheriff was after Railroad Bill, and was about to catch up with him. As the sheriff and his posse ran after Railroad Bill, they came up on a clearing in the woods. Nothing was there except for a black sheep, grazing, who looked up and watched them run by.

Another time, the sheriff followed Bill's tracks into a swamp. He got to a piece of high ground: Railroad Bill's tracks led to it, but didn't lead out.

"I've got him now," the sheriff thought to himself with glee as he drew his big .45. Railroad Bill was wanted dead or alive and the sheriff had had about enough of him alive.

Just then a fox ran by and, before he got out of sight, he turned to the sheriff and laughed. The laugh was eerie —it sounded like the laugh of a human being. The sheriff realized then that Railroad Bill had fooled him again.

The Railroad Bill story that really tickles the Alabama folks, though, is the time the sheriff got a bloodhound posse from a friend over in Mississippi and put them on Bill's trail. There were four dogs, one of them a large, black bloodhound.

After a while, the chase led to a cabin where a pretty girl lived— a girl that the sheriff had heard was Railroad Bill's best girl. The dogs went up to the cabin door but, when the sheriff looked inside, only the girl was there.

The dogs scented something that led away from the cabin, and the sheriff went on. Hours later, the sheriff and his deputies were a mess of skeeter bites and briar scratches. It finally started to get dark and the sheriff headed for home, a mightily discouraged man. When he penned up the dogs, he noticed there were only three.

The next day, the sheriff took the dogs back to Mississippi and asked his friend to bill the county for the dog that got lost. "Just can't understand it," the sheriff said. "Never heard of a bloodhound getting lost."

His friend looked at the sheriff mighty funny. "What the hell do you mean?" he said. "I only lent y'all three dogs."

That's when the sheriff knew old Bill had fooled him again.

Flag Stop

One day old Dr. Rowan, a resident of Beauregard, Mississippi, was walking down the Illinois Central tracks behind his house. The old gentleman, who was in his seventies, was confused by the sudden appearance of a train. Instead of stepping off the tracks to safety, he yelled, "Stop." Of course, the horrified engineer was already trying to stop the train, but it was too late. The old man was run down and killed.

After the death, the old Rowan house was said to be haunted by Dr. Rowan's ghost. Later, in 1926, the phantom began haunting the Illinois Central main line between Hazlehurst and Brookhaven, Mississippi: the tracks where Dr. Rowan died. The ghost would appear with a lantern and flag trains down by giving a danger signal with its light. The ghost would always disappear after flagging a train. So many trains were flagged by the ghost that crews started calling the spot "Flag Stop;" the Illinois Central finally called an unsuccessful investigation of the phenomenon.

The ghost apparently stopped appearing when the dilapidated

Rowan house was torn down in the 1940's. Train crews on the busy Chicago-New Orleans main line must have been relieved to be spared the constant, ghostly delays.

The Railroader's Return

One of the oldest ghost stories known is the return of a loved one at the moment of his or her death. Many a tale-teller has told the story of a wife who looks up to see her husband, who is away at his job or at war; or of a man who sees his far-away mother walk into his room at night. The figure approaches, so close, but then disappears. Soon after, the phone rings or the dread telegram comes.

The return as a notification of death is a common folk tale, and it is no surprise that the annals of American railroading offer several examples of the story. The first comes from Michigan. A mother was sleeping soundly when she was jolted awake. She sat up and flicked on the bedside lamp. Her young son, a railroad brakeman, was standing by her bed wearing overalls and an engineer's cap.

Calmly, too calmly, he told her that he had just slipped and been killed by falling under the wheels of his train. Then, he disappeared. The mother had a bad night, sleeplessly trying to convince herself the apparition was just a bad dream.

In the morning, though, they brought her boy's body home. He had slipped on an icy ladder as he climbed from one car to the next.

Another railroader who returned was Mr. Bryant, a section foreman on the Chesapeake & Ohio Railway's Greenbrier Division in Renick, West Virginia. One night, Bryant was called to clear a land slide. He and his section gang worked late into the night clearing the tracks.

Meanwhile, Mrs. Bryant had cooked a dinner for her husband, knowing he'd be hungry when he returned despite the lateness of the hour. She was sitting in the kitchen reading when she heard him step on the porch and put his lunch pail down with a clang. He usually washed up before coming in, so she started to set out the food.

After a few minutes, her husband still hadn't come into the house. Mrs. Bryant went out to look for him, but no one was there. Just a little while later, a grim neighbor came over to tell her that her husband had been killed on his way home from the slide. The track

The Chicago Great Western, the road Henry Miller worked and died on, was a mid-sized regional railroad in the Midwest. CGW No. 318, a Consolidation (2-8-0), was built by the Rhode Island Locomotive Works in 1901.

car, or speeder, on which he and his crew were riding had wrecked.

Apparently, Mr. Bryant wasn't satisfied with returning just the once. After his widow moved out of the house, the Hardbarger family moved in. They were troubled by singing, lights, steps and, strangest of all, an invisible ghost cat. The family lived in the house for just three years before the eerie manifestations drove them away.

A final story of a railroader's return comes to us from Council Bluffs, Iowa. In this tale, the railroader returns soon after his death, although the woman who saw the spirit already knew of its passing. The tale concerns the ghost of Henry Miller, an engineer on the old Chicago Great Western, who was boarding with his friend E. N. Kattenberg.

On the night of February 8, 1939, Miller seemed to be dogged by bad omens. A pigeon almost flew against the glass as Miller sat by the window. Mrs. Kattenberg felt this was a bad sign, and urged Miller to move. He went in the conservatory to take a nap; the bird followed and perched on window nearest him. Later, as Miller got

Renick, West Virginia during a flood. Mr. Bryant's motor car would have been kept in the section house at the bottom left of the photo.

D17223. OILING UP BEFORE THE START.

Railroading is a hazardous occupation today; think what it was like in the days of steam. Many railroad workers, especially operating employees, were killed or maimed in accidents during railroading's early and middle years.

ready to go out on his run, he hefted his shoes and said they felt unusually heavy. Mrs. Kattenberg lifted them and agreed; she later confided to her husband that this was another bad omen.

Miller's run that night was a fatal one. At about 10:30, he and his firemen were killed in a head-on collision near Tennant, Iowa.

Kattenberg was then on the train opposite Miller; if the accident had been the day before or the day after, he would have been the engineer on the fatal run. He laid off for a few days after the wreck, but returned to work on February 19th. He was understandably cautious, making the run slowly and carefully that night.

When he reached Minneapolis the next morning, Kattenberg called his wife to tell her he was all right. She reported a horrible story. During the night, Henry Miller's ghost had appeared to her, somehow opening her bedroom door and walking through the moonlight to a chair near her bed. The grisly phantom wore the same clothes Miller had on the night of the wreck, but its face was cooked, showing black and scalded in the moonlight.

Ghostly Music

Old railroad grades sometimes stay haunted even after the tracks are pulled up. One of the many rail lines abandoned in recent years was the B&O branch from Ripley Landing through Cottageville to Ripley, West Virginia. The tracks were taken up in 1968.

An old engineer once lived along the tracks in a little house about two miles out of Cottageville. He was a cheery old man who loved the Christmas season. During the holidays, he often played Christmas records on his phonograph and bought candy for the kids in town.

The tracks were abandoned years after he passed away. During the abandonment process, the old man's house was destroyed. The old railroad bed became a neighborhood trail used mainly by hunters.

Two days before Christmas one year, a hunter was driving along

61	Miles.	STATIONS	62
AM			AM
† 8.05	0.0	Lv_____Millwood_____Ar	10.13
f 8.10	1.9	_____Cushings _____	f10.02
f 8.15	2.7	____Cottageville____	f 9.57
f 8.28	6.3	_____Angerona_____	f 9.46
f 8.33	8.0	_____Evans_____	f 9.39
f 8.36	9.0	___Wesley Church___	f 9.35
f 8.39	9.8	_____Parchment_____	f 9.33
8.55	12.3	Ar_____Ripley_____Lv	† 9.25
AM			AM

TABLE 49 — Millwood and Ripley
Westward — Eastward

This 1941 Baltimore & Ohio timetable shows a daily train serving the West Virginia hamlet of Cottageville, where ghostly music is said to play every Christmas season.

the grade, and heard music coming from somewhere back in the trees. Surprised by the phenomenon, he shut off his truck and listened close.

After sitting listening to the music for a little while, he tried to start the truck again. It wouldn't crank. When he looked up from the dash, the hunter saw a man cross the railroad grade and go into a house just to the side. The music started fading and then the house vanished!

The hunter was scared to death. He turned over his car, which started right up, and got out of there. When he told his story later, old folks in the neighborhood said he must have seen the ghost of the old engineer. Folks said the old man had always insisted that guests listen to his records.

A bunch of boys heard the story and drove out along the grade the next night. They didn't see a house or a man, but they did hear strange music. What's more, their cars wouldn't start as long as the music was playing. When it faded, the cars started up like normal.

Locals say that the music only plays on the days just before Christmas. It goes away on Christmas and the grade is silent for another year.

Screaming Jenny

One of America's most famous railroad ghosts is Screaming Jenny, a wraith who has stopped many a Baltimore & Ohio, Chessie System and CSX train on the tracks just west of the station in historic Harpers Ferry, West Virginia. During construction of the Baltimore & Ohio and the Harpers Ferry armory, several storage sheds were built along the B&O tracks west of the station. After construction in the area was finished, the sheds were abandoned. Less fortunate locals found them and sheltered there.

Jenny was one of these poor people. One day, she was huddling close to the tiny fireplace in her shack, trying to warm herself. A spark from the fire lighted on her skirts, which burst into flames. Crazed with fear and pain, Jenny ran from her shack and down the tracks towards the center of Harpers Ferry, screaming wildly for help.

She managed to run almost all the way to the Harpers Ferry train station, a human torch by then, before another tragedy struck. A Baltimore & Ohio train, rounding the curve just west of the station,

Screaming Jenny haunts the ex-B&O track just west of the station and Potomac River bridge in Harpers Ferry, West Virginia. In this photo, the B&O's "Columbian" approaches the Harpers Ferry station from the east.

Bonnie Arant Ertelt

Screaming Jenny.

saw the fiery glow and heard an ungodly scream, but it was too late to stop. The train cut Jenny down and ended her agony.

Or did it? Many a engineer running through Harpers Ferry at night has seen a strange ball of fire on the tracks and has heard a terrible scream. Engineers report slamming on the brakes, stopping too late, then getting down to take what railroaders call "the long walk back" to look for a mangled body. But there is never anything there. That's when the crew realizes that the ghost of the Harpers Ferry tracks, the phantom railroaders call Screaming Jenny, has taken one more horrible trip down the right-of-way.

Dead Man in a Derby Hat

One of America's most well-known narrow-gauge railroads was the Colorado & Southern system (formerly Colorado Central) centered on Denver and serving Leadville, Silver Plume, and Central City. The famous Silver Plume/Central City line ran through Golden and up Clear Creek Canyon.

Colorado Highway 93, Foothills Boulevard, runs north from Boulder to Ralston Creek and beyond. It follows the path of an old Colorado Central line that ran from Golden through Ralston, Colorado. According to local legend, the highway is haunted by the phantom of a man killed by a now-vanished railroad. On July 20, 1881, a Colorado Central train struck a trespasser walking along the Golden-Ralston track near Van Bibber Creek. The man, who was wearing a derby hat, was thrown clear of the tracks. Despite an extensive search for the body, no trace of the man was ever found. Curiously, searchers did find the man's derby hat. It will never be known whether the man dragged himself off into the desert to die or whether his body was seized by coyotes or a mountain lion before searchers could find it.

Whatever his body's fate, the man's spirit seems determined to find it and get it a decent burial. His ghost, one of the most frightening phantoms of the American rails, began appearing soon after the accident. The phantom appeared on trains, along the tracks, and to people passing by Van Bibber Creek. The specter was horrifying—a decomposing corpse, stinking of rotting flesh, wearing the dead man's clothes and derby hat.

With the passage of time, the railroad declined and was replaced

Foothills Boulevard north of Golden, Colorado, home of the dead man in a derby hat.

by today's highway 93. As the years went by, the man in the derby hat's ghost also faded. He still appears to passersby in the Van Bibber Creek area, but now shows himself as a foggy shape or cloud of dust. Instead of the abject terror felt by viewers of a walking corpse, wit-

nesses now report a lingering sense of uneasiness when they encounter the phantom.

Ghost of Mud Cut

One of the greatest challenges facing the builders of the Western North Carolina Railroad, now Norfolk Southern's Salisbury-to-Asheville North Carolina line, was infamous Mud Cut. During construction of the railroad, jelly-like white mud had boiled up in this cut, sometimes raising the track level twenty feet overnight. Thousands of carloads of muck have been taken from this area.

Locals report that Mud Cut is haunted by a unique phantom. The revenant appears as a pair of legs—nothing more—lighted by a lantern the ghost is carrying. The ghostly legs walk up onto the rail-

North Carolina Archives

The Western North Carolina Railroad's Swannanoa Tunnel, near Mud Cut in the North Carolina mountains.

road and then amble down the tracks through Mud Cut to the top of the grade. Once the ghostly legs reach that point, they disappear and then reappear back where they started from.

According to legend, the Mud Cut ghost comes by every night at nine: endlessly appearing, climbing onto the track, walking away, then reappearing in the same spot. Frightened onlookers never see more than the ghost's legs and lantern.

People in the area believe the ghost's nightly walk was started not by a railroad accident but by a family tragedy. According to legend, the ghost is a man named McCathey, an unfortunate who was killed by his brother, Bill McCathey, in a hunting accident. McCathey reportedly mistook his brother for a groundhog and shot him!

McCathey's brother must resent being shot in the place of a lowly groundhog because, as far as anyone knows, his restless spirit still haunts Mud Cut.

SOUTHERN RAILWAY COMPANY'S TRAIN NO. 11, CROSSING THE BLUE RIDGE MOUNTAINS.

"IN THE LAND OF THE SKY."

The ex-Southern Railway line between Salisbury and Asheville is haunted by the Statesville ghost train and the ghost of Mud Cut.

The Southern Railway's (now Norfolk Southern's) famous route from Old Fort to Asheville, North Carolina, shown in this turn-of-the-century post card, is reportedly haunted by the ghost of Mud Cut.

A Western North Carolina Railroad passenger train in Mud Cut.

A Ghostly Race

During the late years of the nineteenth century, a Sioux brave and his black mustang would often race trains rushing across the Western prairies.

Travelers who saw the brave always reported the same thing. The Indian, wearing leopard-spotted war paint, would be seen waiting for the train on an open stretch of prairie. As the train passed him, the Indian would wheel his horse and gallop at full speed after it. It was a race that couldn't be won by flesh and blood. The mustang wouldn't tire but slowly, surely, the train would pull away from the Indian and his horse, finally leaving them far behind.

Was the brave protesting the iron horse's invasion of his land? Or was he simply testing his prowess? No one knows. And no one knows how or when the brave's races ended. Did they end crushed under the wheels of a train?

Bonnie Arant Ertelt

A ghostly race.

Over fifty years later, a drummer was riding a night train from Minneapolis to Butte on the old Northern Pacific. He occupied a lower berth in an old-fashioned sleeper.

The drummer woke with an uneasy feeling. He lay awake for a minute trying to decide what roused him, then thought to open his window shade.

Outside, a lone rider was visible in the darkness. With a sudden shock, the drummer realized the rider was gaining on the train—even though it was highballing at speed across the flat prairie. As the rider drew up to the sleeper window, the drummer strained his eyes trying to see what the horseman looked like.

The rider was an Indian daubed with war paint and mounted on a black mustang. As the drummer watched in disbelief, the Indian and rider passed his car as if they were outrunning the train. Impossible—this couldn't be a real horse and rider.

The same man saw the apparition many other times on the Wyoming or Dakota prairies. He always saw the ghostly horse and rider at night after waking with an uneasy feeling.

Was the Sioux brave returning to test his supernatural powers against the earthly train?

The Ghostly Confederate

The old Western & Atlantic Railroad, scene of the Civil War's Great Locomotive Chase, was also home to a Confederate phantom. Along the old W&A in Georgia, just north of Allatoona Pass, was the grave of a lone Confederate soldier. The man was shot while trying to return across enemy lines to his unit.

Railroaders who worked in the area claimed that the spot was haunted by the ghost of the Confederate hero. The specter reportedly wanders down the tracks with a lantern searching for his fellow soldiers. His dog also returns, and is sometimes seen running in front of a train until it passes the soldier's grave.

The best report of the ghost came from Polly Milan, once an engineer on the run past the grave site. Milan reported that one night, after his train broke in two, he had to walk back by the grave to flag down approaching trains. As he walked past the grave, a ghost appeared, walked towards him, and sat down on the ties. Milan got up enough courage to stammer out some words and try to touch the phantom. He lost his nerve, though, and ran from the resting specter.

The Vanishing Samaritan

One of America's most popular ghost stories is the vanishing hitchhiker: the girl that appears along a road or at a dance, is given a ride by a man to her home, and then disappears. The man goes to the door, a mother or father answers, and the man finds that the girl died years ago on that day. Several railroad ghost stories are related to the vanishing hitchhiker and may represent earlier forms of the story, forms popular before the coming of the automobile.

One of these is the Vanishing Samaritan of Willis, Ohio. One night, a group of railroad men was gathered around a fire in a shack near the Willis roundhouse. The old hostler mentioned he was once a hobo, but had settled down in Willis, married, and stayed on.

One of the men asked how the hostler came to give up hoboing. The old man told how he had jumped off a freight in the Willis yard one night in the rain. He heard a voice call, "Bad rain tonight, isn't it?"

The voice was friendly, but the hobo worried it was a yard bull trying to latch onto him. He stayed quiet and peered into the dark, trying to see who it was.

A man dressed in a raincoat and hat walked up. "You got anywhere to stay?" he asked the hobo.

"No, sir," the hobo said, "and I'd sure appreciate a bite to eat."

"Just follow me on home," the man said. "We'll fix you up."

The two walked off together. The man in the raincoat didn't seem interested in talking, so the hobo kept his mouth shut, too. After two or three blocks, they reached the man's house. "Just go on in," the man said.

The 'bo assumed the man was going around back to take off his rain things or some such, so he walked on in. There was a lady with a lot of children in the house. The hobo sat down at the table and waited and waited. The man never came back.

"Your husband said I could get some dinner here," the hobo finally said.

"Sure thing," the woman said. She fixed up a great big dinner for the 'bo and he ate.

"You can have the upstairs room," the woman said after the hobo finished his food. The man still wasn't back.

"Your man o.k.?" the hobo asked. "I could go out and look for him."

The woman smiled. "He's always bringing tramps home on rainy nights," she said. "And I always take care of them for him. He was a railroad man, got killed up there in the yard six years ago." The old hostler gazed into the fire, still remembering. "She didn't seem bothered about it at all," he said, "but I didn't sleep much that night, I can tell you. I figured somebody up there was trying to tell me something, so I stopped tramping the next day."

Bill McKeon's Ghost

In March 1888, New York Central engineer Bill McKeon accepted a call to work a snow-plow train on the railroad's Batavia to North Tonawanda branch. There had already been two wrecks on the branch that winter and Bill was reluctant to take the run. An old railroad superstition said that accidents always come in groups of three.

McKeon told his fireman, Fred Hunt, that he had a terrible feel-

Engineer Bill McKeon's ghost would not lie quiet in North Tonowanda graveyard.

ing that the third wreck was coming and that it was going to get him. Hunt told McKeon not to worry, that nothing would happen unless his number was up. "If your number is up," Hunt went on, "there's nothing you can do about it anyway."

Bill McKeon's number ran out the next day. As he ran the snowplow extra down the icy tracks, the engine plunged off the rails just as Bill pulled out his watch to check the time. The engine churned into Black Ash Swamp and McKeon died at the throttle; he was buried in the North Tonawanda graveyard. Hunt survived the wreck and continued to fire for the New York Central.

One year after the tragedy, farmers in the Black Ash Swamp area began to report a frightening apparition: a ghost with a lantern stalking the scene of McKeon's wreck at night. Folks began to say that the phantom was Bill McKeon's ghost.

If you believe the locals, the phantom was busy during the next month. A man reported seeing a monster with glowing eyes swinging a lantern at the wreck scene. One train crew was delayed because they were afraid to run down the apparition as it walked the track. Another engineer ran right over the specter, only to see it disappear with a terrible scream. Most folks, though, just reported a mysterious light glowing in the swamp.

Bill McKeon's reappearance seemed to follow a regular annual pattern. The phantom railroader would appear every year on the anniversary of McKeon's wreck, then make nightly appearances for a month, fading away after that until the next wreck anniversary.

The stories got wilder and wilder. McKeon's ghost was said to cause shooting stars and a blood-red moon. A local farmer reported that the moon-eyed, lantern-carrying monster invaded his barn.

Finally, Fred Hunt got a feeling about the whole thing. "He's looking for his watch," the fireman claimed. Local railroaders, including Hunt himself, made inquiries in the community and found that a man had picked the watch up at the scene of the fatal wreck. The stemwinder was retrieved from the ghoul.

One cold March evening, during McKeon's annual month of revisits to mother Earth, Hunt and some other local railroaders placed the watch in the snow at the wreck site, right alongside the branch-line rails. The men then waited to see what would happen.

Observers reported an eerie sight. The lantern-carrying phantom did walk the tracks that night. When it reached the watch, the ghost stopped and seemed to stoop down to pick up the stemwinder. Then, the timepiece arrowed into the air like a rocket, finally disappearing from sight as it shot straight up into space. Neither the ghost nor the watch was ever seen again.

The Ghostly Lovers

For whatever reason, West Virginia and North Carolina seem to be the states with the most ghostly train stories. Another chiller from West Virginia concerns the B&O line from Morgantown to Rowlesburg.

It seems that once, many years ago, a Rowlesburg woman was earning money by working in Pittsburgh as a domestic. While living in Pittsburgh, she began dating a young man from her hometown area and fell in love.

She thought he loved her too, but when she found she was pregnant, the young man refused to marry her. So, alone and in trouble,

The railroad along the Cheat River near Rowlesburg, West Virginia, the Morgantown & Kingwood, was the setting for the mysterious tale of the misty ghost lovers. M&K No. 14, built by Baldwin in 1909, was used on the line.

Cascade Falls, along the ex-Morgantown & Kingwood/Baltimore & Ohio line from Morgantown to Rowlesburg, West Virginia.

the only thing she could do was go home to her family in disgrace.

As she rode homeward, she started to think about the horror of her position. She wasn't even sure if her family would take her, an unwed mother-to-be, in.

She was almost home—the train was following the Cheat River north of Rowlesburg. The girl went out on the platform to get some air. It was a beautiful night lit by a full moon.

The train was passing some caverns along the river. The girl, still out on the platform, looked down the embankment into the rushing waters. Feeling desolate and hopeless, she jumped.

The young man was crushed with shame when he heard of his girlfriend's suicide. Soon afterward, he went home too.

The B&O's M&K Subdivision west of Rowlesburg, West Virginia was the scene of twin suicides committed by a pair of young lovers. Their bodies, found in the rushing waters of the Cheat River, are said to reappear as mists rising from the river below the railroad.

Morgantown & Kingwood No. 7, a 2-8-0 built in 1903, with a group of trainmen. This engine might well have pulled the trains mentioned in the story of the ghostly lovers and their return to Rowlesburg, West Virginia.

On the year anniversary of her death, he went to the caverns along the river. He was found days later, drowned on the bottom of the Cheat River across from the spot where the girl killed herself.

Old railroad men say that, on the night of the full moon, the ghost of the dead girl rises as a cold white mist. It hovers for a minute until another mist rises from the Cheat River. The mists merge together, drift upward and fade away.

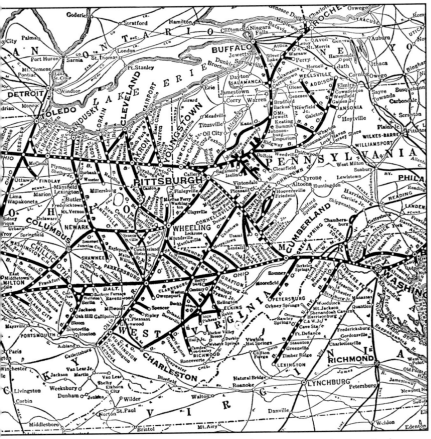

The former Baltimore & Ohio, shown in this 1941 map, is America's most-haunted railroad. Most of the phantoms along its tracks are West Virginia natives.

The Phantom of Lewiston Narrows

Lewiston Narrows is a remote wilderness in Pennsylvania's Allegheny Mountains. The old Pennsylvania Railroad ran through the Narrows, bounded on one side by a road, a canal and the Juniata River, on the other by a sheer cliff. The jagged rocks of Black Log Mountain brooded over the whole scene.

The "Pittsburgh and Northern Express" was running through the narrows during the early morning hours of August 31, 1909, when the crack of an exploding track torpedo signalled the engineer to stop. When the express ground to a halt, a lone figure with a gun demanded entrance to the baggage car.

The eerie robber was clad in a black hat draped with loose cloth

The phantom of Lewiston Narrows haunted trackside, seeking a bag of gold.

Lewiston Narrows.

that covered most of his body. After a hurried look through the baggage car, he absconded with a money sack stuffed with $65 worth of new pennies. He made a bad choice: he left a half-million dollar bundle of notes in the car.

A pack of hounds brought in to search the area refused to follow the bandit's scent. As the years went by, local people began to report a phantom, clad all in black, walking the track at the scene of the robbery or lurking among the cliffs of Black Log Mountain. People believed the figure was the Lewiston Narrows phantom, still looking for the valuable loot that had eluded him.

The White Woman of Silver Run

The B&O engineer, a young man, was proud to be on the westbound express run that evening. His train was leaving Grafton, West Virginia for Clarksburg and Parkersburg.

The express made the Clarksburg, West Virginia stop without incident and was off again. The train was nearing Silver Run Tunnel when the engineer saw a woman in a white gown standing on the track. She was lit by the headlight and the half moon overhead. The engineer threw the brakes into emergency and the train screeched to a halt.

The engineer knew he couldn't stop in time and he prayed the woman would jump off the tracks. Suddenly, she seemed to just glide down the track away from the engine. As the train came to a stop, the engineer and fireman jumped off and ran toward the woman. She disappeared into a fog bank that blanketed the track ahead.

The train's conductor came running up, wondering about the cause of the emergency stop. He and the engineer searched the tracks ahead. They found nothing, so they took the train on its way again.

The young engineer had the run every other night. He asked around and found that the other man on the run had never seen the woman. By the time of his next run, the young engineer was thinking he might just have seen a patch of fog or some such.

The express was running towards Silver Run Tunnel that night with the young engineer at the throttle when the woman in white appeared again. This time, as if to prove she was real, the young

The stately Baltimore & Ohio station in Grafton, West Virginia, was an crew-change point on the Monongah Division for many years. The engineers who encountered the "white woman of Silver Run" may have reported for duty here, prior to their 105-mile run to Parkersburg.

man could see many details about her—golden slippers, jet black hair, a jeweled brooch pinned to the neckline of her dress. The engineer put the train into emergency again.

When the train stopped, the engineer, fireman and conductor again searched for the woman. She had disappeared and they could find no trace of her.

The crew was afraid to delay the express any longer, so the engineer blew a warning whistle and the train started off again.

After that, the woman in white didn't appear for a month or so—until the next half moon. As the train approached the tunnel that night, the woman was standing at her usual spot. The young engineer stopped the train, then blew the whistle and started off again. This time, there was a new manifestation—the whistle was answered by a horrible moan.

This third delay was too much, and the once-proud young engineer was put back on a freight run. A new engineer, O'Flannery, was put on the express.

For a month, O'Flannery made the run without incident. Then he saw the woman, too.

The express's fireman told the young engineer all about it. It was a clear autumn night. The engineer saw the woman, made an emergency stop, and ran after her. She disappeared into a fog bank, the only fog the crew had sighted that evening. The fog bank then quickly faded.

O'Flannery was rattled, the fireman said. He thought he saw the woman on the track after the train started up again, then he thought he saw her once when the fireman opened the firebox doors. He left the engine that night muttering he'd run the woman down if he ever sighted her again.

O'Flannery's next run was one that was long remembered on the B&O. The fireman told the young engineer about it. It seems that O'Flannery did see the woman in white that night and didn't stop. He ran right over her ghostly form.

She seemed to disappear, but when the train got to Parkersburg, the crew found they were the subject of a lot of talk. The woman in white had been sighted by signalmen, agents and section men from the tunnel all the way to Parkersburg, sitting gracefully on the engine's cowcatcher!

The men in the Parkersburg tower reported they saw the woman on the cowcatcher as the train approached. They said that, as it slowed for the station, the express passed through a patch of fog and the woman simply disappeared. O'Flannery had a nervous breakdown and was off the board for quite a while.

The railroad company was getting worried about all the talk and some railroad agents made inquiries. They found that a woman had disappeared from the express twenty-five years earlier. She was on her way to Parkersburg to meet her fiancee, but never arrived. She was never heard of again.

Many years later, the young engineer—now getting old—heard the skeleton of a woman had been found by workmen digging a cel-

Two Baltimore & Ohio passenger trains at the division point and junction in Parkersburg, West Virginia in 1920. According to legend, men working in the Parkersburg tower saw the "white woman of Silver Run" disappear.

lar under an old house near Silver Run Tunnel. After that, the White Woman of Silver Run was never seen again. But old timers say you could still hear her when the half moon hung low over the hills. Nights like that, when a train whistled near the tunnel at midnight, the whistle was answered by a woman's moan.

This segment of the B&O's mainline to St. Louis was abandoned by successor CSX in the mid-1980's.

The Dancing Woman of Manuelito

The White Woman of Silver Run might be called a flirtatious ghost. She's a rare creature: most revenants seem to care little about what the living think of them.

Another example of a vivacious female ghost is the Dancing Woman of Manuelito. Manuelito is a hamlet along the Santa Fe's tracks just west of Gallup, New Mexico. Like the ghostly Confederate soldier of Allatoona Pass, Manuelito's ghost is connected to a track-side grave. The grave in question was beside the east switch at Manuelito, and was the last resting place for a Mexican woman murdered by her husband.

Local Hispanics long claimed that the grave site was haunted by the murdered woman. The wraith was said to dance on her own grave.

Battle of the Dead

The Southern Pacific "Slim Princess" narrow-gauge, running from Laws to Keeler, California, was one of the last operating narrow-gauge railroads in the United States. At its extreme Southern end, the little railroad ran along the east shore of dry Owens Lake from Mt. Whitney Station—near Lone Pine, California—to Keeler.

According to local legend, passengers aboard one of the Southern Pacific narrow-gauge trains once witnessed a ghostly battle between Paiute Indians and U. S. Cavalry. The train was traveling along the Owens Lake bed at the time; it was broad daylight outside. Witnesses reported hearing the sounds of the battle—screams, gunshots—and seeing both troopers and Indians fall dead and wounded.

Curiously, the area was the scene of a battle between Paiutes and

Southern Pacific narrow-gauge 4-6-0 No. 8 at Keeler, California on March 1, 1948. Passengers riding the Southern Pacific narrow-gauge near Keeler saw the battle of the dead.

cavalry many years before. The phantom battle has never reappeared, and today the "Slim Princess" is just a memory. The historic railroad was abandoned in 1960.

The Phantom Lantern of Ray City

Between Valdosta and Nashville, Georgia, the ex-Southern Railway line runs through the hamlet of Ray City, Georgia. In Ray City, a dirt road runs from City Hall back towards the railroad tracks.

At one time, a black railroader noticed a school bus stalled on the tracks at Ray City. A train was approaching; the man grabbed his lantern and signalled it to stop. The train braked in time to save the children, but the man stayed on the tracks too long. The train hit and killed him.

Today, folks around Ray City say that, if you drive down that dirt road to the end and wait there, right by the tracks, you can sometimes see the old black man's ghost waving his lantern, still trying to stop the train. Folks say that you're most likely to see the old man if you go down and watch on a night with a full moon.

The Conductor's Ghost

Not far from Bostian's Bridge, on the old Western North Carolina Railroad line from Salisbury to Asheville, is Statesville, North Carolina. The Southern Railway, the eventual owner of the Western North Carolina Railroad, also had branches from Statesville northwest to Taylorsville and south to Mooresville.

The Mooresville line ran through the hamlet of Barium Springs and the small town of Troutman. Between Statesville and Barium Springs, near Amity Hill Road, the branch crossed Third Creek on a high trestle.

According to local legend, a railway conductor once fell off the bridge to his death. Since then, the ghost of the unfortunate railroader has reappeared on the anniversary of his death. People who visit the bridge on that day report seeing the conductor's ghost swinging his lantern.

The old branch has been abandoned back from Mooresville to just north of Troutman. The tracks still run from Statesville south across the trestle and through Barium Springs but they see little, if any, use.

Villa Main Grade Crossing Phantoms

One of the most famous railroad hauntings of recent years is the ghosts of the Villa Main Street grade crossing near San Antonio, Texas. The haunting legend developed as the result of a horrendous freight train-school bus collision at the grade crossing. A number of children were killed, and streets in the area were named after those who died as a memorial.

According to residents of the neighborhood, the ghosts of the dead children return to guard the crossing. They are invisible, and manifest themselves by moving cars stopped across the tracks at the Villa Main crossing to safety. Many drivers have described the eerie experience of having their car rolled forward from the crossing by an unseen force.

One curiosity seeker covered her car with flour before stopping near the grade crossing in an attempt to find visible evidence of the ghosts. According to witnesses, small hand prints appeared in the flour covering the car's windshield.

Death in Georgia

In Bloodville, Georgia before the turn of the century, a black man was staggering home on a Saturday night. Missing the underpass taking a road below the railroad tracks, he stumbled up onto the right-of-way. He fell and was too dead drunk to get up.

Imagine the man's woozy terror as he heard the night train whistle for the crossing. He tried desperately to crawl to safety but, before he could, the train hit him and ground him to bloody pulp.

After that terrible night, the train and the man returned every week to meet their appointment with death. According to Bloodville residents, every Saturday midnight brought two screams from the man followed by one blast of the train's whistle. Curiously, these sounds of the tragedy were followed by a ghostly voice speaking the word, "thumb." There's no explaining the actions of the dead.

Phantom Tracklayers at Sinks of Dove Creek

Sinks of Dove Creek is the site of an old Central Pacific labor camp once used by the Chinese workers who built the first transcontinental railroad across California, Nevada, and Utah.

During the late 1970s, a park ranger was participating in a historic reenactment at Sinks of Dove Creek. The ranger and his friends were dressed in authentic Army uniforms like those used by the Twenty-

This old engraving depicts a Central Pacific Railroad train running across its newly built right-of-way through the "alkali desert." The original Central Pacific line near Sinks of Dove Creek must have looked much like this.

First Infantry, the Army unit assigned to protect the Central Pacific workers back in the 1860's.

The ranger had two to five a.m. guard duty at the reenactment camp. He patrolled back and forth along the abandoned Central Pacific grade running above the encampment. The other men were all asleep.

Dying campfires flickered below, reflecting off the encampment tents. The guard found himself thinking how time was almost reversed, how everything looked just as it must have during the building of the transcontinental railroad.

That's when he heard the sound, a muffled roar off in the distance. Suddenly a far-off light, like that of a kerosene lantern, appeared swinging side-to-side across the old grade.

As it got closer, the ranger could make the roaring out more clearly. It sounded like a steam engine approaching him down the old grade, although there was nothing to be seen.

Then, it was running right over him. The ranger couldn't believe his ears. He couldn't see it, couldn't feel it, but he could hear the old steam engine as clearly as if it was 1869 again.

Rattled by the uncanny experience, the ranger made his way back to camp. He sat huddled in front of a fire near the tents, trying to calm himself. Finally, he decided to stay out his guard duty no matter what happened. He walked back up onto the old Central Pacific grade.

This time, his experience was different. He was surrounded by whispers and soft footsteps. Overcoming his fear enough to listen closely, the ranger realized the voices were speaking in Chinese. One word he kept hearing was "A-melican, A-melican." The hair rose on his neck and arms when he realized the invisible Central Pacific workers were talking about him.

The ranger thought about the sounds. He knew that the soldiers of the Twenty-First Infantry had protected Chinese workers in this very camp. Had the reenactment turned back the pages of time in some way?

The ranger shook his head, then concentrated again on the ghostly noises all around him. He heard railroad work sounds—the dull thuds of spikes being hammered into ties, the soft footsteps of Chinese workers and the heavy tread of Anglos.

As he looked down the grade, the ranger saw an eerie sight. The grade was covered with pinpricks of light. As he watched the spectacle, he realized the lights must be sparks glancing from spikes and rails as the ghostly workers hammered down the Central Pacific track —an event that happened a hundred and ten years before!

After his experience, the ranger became fascinated with the history of the Sinks of Dove Creek area, which is near Kelton, Utah and the Golden Spike National Historic Site. He talked with people who hunt in the area and learned that they knew of the ghostly workers; that he wasn't the only person who'd ever witnessed the phenomena.

Many people were reluctant to use the dirt road that follows the old grade. They believed the ghost train might run them down. Others had heard the voices of the phantom workers. The ranger even unearthed stories old railroad engineers told about the time when the track running by Sinks of Dove Creek was still in use. Engineers had heard ghost trains coming towards them on their runs through the desert near Sinks of Dove Creek.

Some of the ghost trains had even carried lights, unnerving the train crews, who would prepare for a terrible collision. When the real train made its emergency stop, the other train would keep coming despite efforts to warn it. Then the ghost train would pass right over the real train, headlight blaring and engine sound puffing away, and disappear off into the desert night.

The ranger examined the encampment, too, and realized that the men doing the reenactment had camped right on top of an old Chinese work camp. The dugouts that had served as the bottoms of the Chinese laborers' huts were right there. When the ranger looked through the dugouts, the hair on his neck and arms stood up again. He could feel the ghost workers there.

What trick of time keeps the ghost workers struggling with spikes and rails at the Sinks of Dove Creek labor camp?

The Ghost of Doe River Gorge

The East Tennessee and Western North Carolina Railroad, the mountaineers' beloved Tweetsie, was built through the highlands of Tennessee and North Carolina during the late 1800's and early 1900's. At its greatest extent, the railroad ran from Johnson City, Tennessee to Boone, North Carolina.

The little narrow gauge was no match for modern roads. The line was abandoned back to Cranberry, North Carolina in 1940, and back to Elizabethton, Tennessee in 1950. The 1950 abandonment meant the end of rail service through breathtaking Doe River Gorge, one of the most scenic, least known, and least accessible natural wonders east of the Mississippi.

Today, the Gorge is almost impossible to access; only snakes, bears and very hardy humans see its splendors. The Gorge still has rails, laid down by a short-lived scenic railroad two decades ago, but no trains have run there in many years.

According to old Tweetsie workers, the Gorge is haunted by the ghost of a workman killed there. One of the most unusual things about the Doe River Gorge Ghost is that his name, Dave Gourley, has come down to us.

Gourley, who worked in the Gorge, was drying himself by a fire after a rainstorm. Also nearby, unfortunately, were dynamite and blasting caps. The unstable caps exploded from the heat, detonating the dynamite and killing Gourley. After Gourley's death, Tweetsie trainmen say they always saw his ghost walking the tracks in the Gorge if they went through on a night run.

The tracks are still there, but few people ever get the chance to see the Ghost of Doe River Gorge walk the line today.

Fight on the Spur

Years ago, the Shenandoah and Susquehanna Railroad was building a spur to a lumber camp in Pennsylvania. During the construction of the branch, two of the track workers fought and one of them was killed.

For years after the fight, men who worked on the railroad or in the lumber camp would see the grisly aftermath of the conflict reenacted: the winning track worker would appear, pushing the dead man along the tracks in a wheel barrow. The dead man's feet would be seen hanging over one side of the wheel barrow, while his head lolled over the other.

The Shake City Ghost

The California Western Railroad is a short line that operates

East Tennessee & Western North Carolina trackage in Doe River Gorge, 1906. It is here that the ghost of Doe River Gorge is said to appear.

Above: ET&WNC No. 10 and train exit Doe River Gorge running eastbound to Cranberry, North Carolina, circa 1940. The following photo was taken at the same spot in 1980.

Tony Reevy

Right: The entrance to Doe River Gorge, along the abandoned East Tennessee & Western North Carolina Railroad grade near Hampton, Tennessee.

excursions through the redwood forests of northern California. The line runs forty miles inland from Fort Bragg, on the Pacific Coast, to Willits, California. Built as a logging railroad in 1885, the line inaugurated steam passenger service in 1904.

The railroad's passenger trains are known as "Skunks" after the smelly diesel rail cars that provide passenger service when the line is not operating full-fledged trains. The California Western has used the rail cars since 1925.

The California Western is important to local residents as well as tourists as it passes through areas that are difficult to access by road. One of the railroad's rural stops is known as Shake City.

The platform at Shake City is said to be haunted by a ghostly figure that appears late on winter evenings. Local legend in this town of a few dozen people says the ghost is the phantom of an elderly man who slipped off the platform and died from his injuries.

Local folklore goes on to say that the man was on his way to Fort Bragg to begin his life anew on the Pacific Coast. Folks say that the man is waiting for another train so that he can finish the trip.

Ghost of the New York Subway

Few trains are as prosaic as the trains of the gloomy New York

Railroad Museum of Pennsylvania

California Western saddle tank No. 7 (later No. 17), built by Baldwin in 1909.

City subway. Yet even these everyday conveyances are said to be

Tony Reevy

Shake City, a lonely siding on the California Western Railroad, is said to be haunted by the ghost of a passenger.

Present-day California Western excursion train.

haunted.

The ghost of the New York subway, an etherial white figure, materializes near the Hoyt-Schermerhorn station. The ghost appears in and out of the tunnel in a way that would be impossible for any living being. Sometimes the ghost is seen just as a subway train enters the station.

If there is an explanation for why the ghost appears, it has been lost.

The Irishman of White Lick Creek

The old railroad bridge across White Lick Creek, near Danville, Indiana, is gone now. The old New York Central line that once crossed it is abandoned.

The line was abandoned despite an interesting history. One of the first lines constructed in that part of the state, the track was built by Irish laborers during a railroad boom in the 1850's.

Local folklore says that during the construction of the White Lick Creek bridge, an Irish laborer fell to his death into one of the trestle piers. Rather than slow the construction to pull his body out, he was simply sealed up in the pier and left there.

After just a few years went by, weird stories began to be told about the bridge. People began to fear that the ghost of the dead Irishman was returning to the site of his death and entombment. They didn't like what was oozing out of the support, for one thing. Water dripped from it even during the driest summer season, water that rolled down the pier slowly—like human tears. Sometimes folks even saw a red liquid, blood-like, dripping from the support into the creek below.

Folks were afraid to go near the place at all the first night of each full moon. That was when people saw the dead Irishman's specter standing on the bridge —a skeleton with a lighted lantern in its hand. When a train whistled, the ghost would wave the lantern. People even say that the ghost would scream at the trains, imploring the crew to stop and take him aboard so his soul could rest in peace.

No train stopped to carry the Irishman's soul away. Today, the track he labored and died to build is gone and nothing but a memory. The bridge is gone, too, but people say that the Irishman still waits at the old bridge site, lantern in his bony hand, for the train to heaven that will never come.

Two Ghost Tramps

As mentioned above, ghost tramps are one of the rarities of railroad folklore. Here are the only ghost tramp stories found in the research for this book, both from the well-haunted state of West Virginia.

The Collier Ghost Tramp

The first ghostly tramp story concerns a man who had just moved to Collier, West Virginia. This man was sitting on his back porch one evening when he saw a drunken hobo walk down the nearby railroad tracks, taking great swigs from a bottle.

The hobo sat down upon the rails. The man looked on with a growing sense of alarm, as a train was due through town at 9:15 p.m.

Finally, just after nine, the man's wife went out on the porch to join him. She too saw the drunken hobo, and urged her husband to run down to the tracks, which were about a quarter-mile away, and warn the tramp.

The man ran toward the tracks, shouting a warning. The old tramp, who seemed so drunk that he was insensible, still sat on the rails. The man heard an engine wail close by, and knew he would be too late to save the hobo. The engine's headlight shone on the rails, casting a wash of light over the doomed little figure huddled on the right-of-way. And then, just before the train hit the tramp, he disappeared. The man stopped short in astonishment.

Later, he asked his new landlord about the ghost tramp. Instead of being laughed at, like he expected, he heard an incredible story. The old tramp, a stranger, was driven from town by the people of Collier. Then, he sat down on the rails at the edge of town to wait for a train to ride. A train ran over him and killed him right there. Since then, the tramp had reappeared every year on the anniversary of his death, terrifying the townspeople. The newcomer was the first person who had dared to go near the ghost.

The tramp never returned to Collier. Apparently, he had been waiting for someone who cared enough to try and save him rather than just leave him to his fate.

Ghost Tramp of the Cleveland Special

In 1919, a hobo named Lantz stood by the tracks in Cleveland, Ohio, waiting to hop the 11:15 p.m. "Cleveland Special" back to his hometown of Rowlesburg, West Virginia.

After a few minutes, he looked around and spotted an older hobo squatting by the tracks. He walked over to the other 'bo, and asked him where he was going.

The 'bo replied, in an oddly emotionless voice, that he was going to Rowlesburg, West Virginia. Lantz was delighted to find a traveling partner and said so.

The other hobo simply said, "You aren't going to be on the 11:15."

Lantz argued but the other 'bo just sat there, saying, "No, you won't be on the 11:15." The old 'bo never even looked at Lantz.

When the 11:15 whistled in the distance, the old hobo stood up with his back to Lantz and got ready to hop the train. Lantz stood up, too. Without turning, the old hobo said, "That train will cause your death."

The Baltimore & Ohio depot at Rowlesburg, West Virginia, deep in the Mountain State, is the site of a notable ghost tramp story.

Lantz stared at the man, and noticed that his red and green plaid shirt was soaked with blood. He looked away and, next thing he knew, the other man leaned right over and yelled in his ear, "You aren't going on this train, mister."

Turning quickly, Lantz looked the stranger full in the face for the first time. What he saw was horrible: the man's face was deeply scratched, bloody, and partially crushed. Lantz grabbed at the creature, but his hands went right through the bloody wreck's plaid shirt. Lantz screamed and fainted.

When Lantz awoke, the bloody hobo was gone. He hopped the next train out and made it to Rowlesburg o.k. He noticed a commotion around the depot when he got in.

"What's going on?" he asked the depot janitor.

"Oh, a hobo tried to jump off the 'Cleveland Special' and got cut to bits. All that's left of him is pieces wrapped in a plaid shirt."

Lantz felt sick to his stomach. "Red and green plaid?" he asked softly.

The janitor stared at him. "How in the hell did you know?" he asked.

The East Portal of much-haunted Hoosac Tunnel is depicted in this World War I-era postcard.

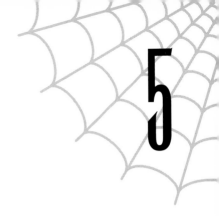

Haunted Tunnels

t is no surprise that many railroad tunnels are reportedly haunted. Tunnels—dark, damp, dangerous, often the scene of tragedies—are just the sort of places that supernatural legends grow up around.

It helps hauntings, too, that many lives were lost in building America's railroad tunnels, and many more in inspecting and maintaining them down through the years. Several of our haunted tunnel legends perpetuate memories of the sacrifices working men made to allow the trains to go through. The most famous of these ghostly workers and, like Railroad Bill, a legend in his own right, is John Henry.

John Henry and Big Bend Tunnel

"John Henry was a very small boy,

Fell on his mammy's knee;

Picked up a hammer and a little piece of steel,

'Lord, a hammer'll be the death of me,

Lord, a hammer'll be the death of me.'"

"John Henry," American folk song.

John Henry, the famous steel-driving man, probably worked in West Virginia's Big Bend Tunnel, near Hinton, West Virginia. Hinton is on the old Chesapeake and Ohio (now CSX) line that runs past White Sulfur Springs, West Virginia, and then through the New River Gorge. The Big Bend Tunnel was constructed between 1870 and 1873 as part of the Chesapeake & Ohio's line from Richmond to

Cincinnati. Building the Big Bend Tunnel was a terrible job: the rock was unstable and many workers died.

According to legend, it was in the tunnel that John Henry fought and won his famous contest with the steam drill, dying from a stroke soon afterwards. The popular folk song "John Henry" remains as a monument to the strength of this man, who could beat a machine drill down.

Since the contest, railroad workers have reported seeing a ghost inside the bore, near the east portal. When the ghost appears, the clang, clang, clang of a hammer is heard first. Then the shadowy figure of a giant man can be seen driving a drill into the tunnel wall, swinging a hammer in each hand. At other times, just the sound of the hammer can be heard. Occasionally a huge ghostly figure is seen walking through the tunnel, a hammer in each hand.

The ghost reportedly first appeared soon after John Henry's death, when the tunnel was still under construction. Many of the African-American construction workers refused to labor in the tunnel for a time after the tragedy, claiming they had heard John Henry's ghost driving steel in the bore.

The original Big Bend Tunnel was superseded by a new, parallel bore with larger clearances built in 1932. In 1974, the old Big Bend Tunnel was closed to traffic and the rails removed. The 1932 tunnel is still in use by freight trains and Amtrak's "Cardinal". Now that the old Big Bend Tunnel is unused, does John Henry still return to the scene of his victory over the steam drill?

Hoosac Tunnel Ghosts

Like Indiana's Big Tunnel (see below), Massachusetts' Hoosac Tunnel is haunted by a bewildering array of ghosts. And, if any stretch of railroad in the United States deserves to be haunted, Hoosac Tunnel does. Still one of the longest tunnels in America, built between 1856 and 1875 at the cost of $20,000,000 and 195 lives, the 4 ¾ mile bore killed many a man. Nicknamed the "Great Bore" and the "bloody pit," the tunnel was the scene of hard work and too-frequent horror.

The tunnel was also the scene of the first American use of nitroglycerin for blasting, and eventually consumed an incredible 500,000 pounds of the dangerous liquid. Two deaths caused by a nitro blast in 1865, and the mysterious death of the man responsible for the blast a year later, are the most common explanation for the hauntings in Hoosac Tunnel.

The most common ghostly manifestation in Hoosac Tunnel is a man's voice groaning and crying in pain. The frightening noise was first reported soon after the death of the nitro killer, Ringo Kelley, in 1866.

The noise is documented in records dating back to September 1868. If hard rock, nitro and seeping water were not enough to contend with, the miners building the tunnel encountered gas. Thirteen workers boring a shaft were killed when a gas explosion destroyed the pumping station keeping their work-site free of water. The doomed men built a raft to float up to the surface on the rising water, but were suffocated by the gas. The shaft, its top clogged by debris from the explosion, soon filled with water. The dead men were not found for over a year.

While the men were missing, strange, new manifestations were reported. Eerie shapes were seen and far-away wails heard near the water-logged shaft. Fellow workers saw the missing miners carrying their work tools through a cloud of fog and snow.

After the dead men's bodies were recovered, these wraiths ceased to appear. The painful moaning in the tunnel's main bore continued, however. Now, it was accompanied by the form of a headless workman with a lantern, lighted an unearthly blue. The ghost floated along just above the tunnel's rock floor, and brought an earthly chill along with it.

The tunnel ghosts started to jeopardize the lives of the living. In 1874, a local hunter was reportedly forced into Hoosac Tunnel by ghostly shapes that then beat him with his own gun. A tunnel watchman bringing firewood into the tunnel in 1875 turned his cart around suddenly and galloped out of the bore. His horses and cart were later found in the woods near the tunnel, but the watchman had vanished.

In recent years, the tunnel ghosts are more often said to guard the living than to endanger them. One ex-Boston & Maine railroad man reports that, on two occasions, ghosts in the tunnel saved his life while he was working there. They told him to run when he didn't notice an approaching train, and to drop a crowbar just before it was charged by 11,000 volts from a short-circuited power line. The same worker reported hearing a strange laugh during an incident in which he was almost killed by a falling oak tree. Others have reported seeing the blue-lighted figure first encountered in 1872 and hearing strange, far-away voices in the tunnel. Many who have visited the tunnel report a strange feeling of foreboding and dread permeating the "Great Bore."

The tunnel is a very unsafe place to visit, especially because of the heavy train traffic through it and its great length. Visitors to the Berkshire Hills may learn more about Hoosac Tunnel by visiting the Hoosac Tunnel Museum in North Adams, Massachusetts' Western Gateway Heritage State Park.

Cowee Tunnel

During the mid-1850s, the Western North Carolina Railroad began snaking its way westward from Salisbury, North Carolina. It reached Asheville about twenty-five years later, its progress slowed by the Civil War, Reconstruction, and the complications involved in building a rail line over the mountains west of Old Fort, North Carolina. Most of the line was built by convicts provided by the state.

The Western North Carolina didn't stop at Asheville. It continued to push west and, by the early 1880's, the line had reached the spot now known as Dillsboro, North Carolina. Its next target was Bryson City, North Carolina, sixteen miles farther west. A hairpin turn in the Tuckasegee River stood in the way and the railroad decided to bypass it with a tunnel. The new tunnel, Cowee Tunnel, was on the other side of the river from the convicts' camp. They were ferried over every day, still chained into work gangs, in an old flatboat.

One winter day in 1883, the river was a mad torrent. As a gang of twenty convicts was being ferried across, the boat capsized. Imagine the men, chained to each other with heavy ankle irons, struggling and sinking in the rushing river. Only one of the twenty survived. The other nineteen are buried on a hillside above the river.

Today, Cowee Tunnel is said to be haunted by the ghosts of the drowned convicts. Excursion trains of the Great Smoky Mountains Railway run through the tunnel, the car hosts explaining the legend as they go. The convicts' ghosts are said to make eerie cries in the tunnel, especially when a train is passing through.

To hear more about the Cowee Tunnel ghosts, ride the Tuckasegee River Excursion on the Great Smoky Mountains Railway. The excursion runs from Dillsboro to Bryson City, North Carolina and return. Trains run most of the year, except in the dead of winter.

The Many Ghosts of Big Tunnel

If North Carolina and West Virginia hold awards for the states with the most railroad ghosts, the Baltimore & Ohio holds the award for the most haunted railroad.

Another of the many B&O phantoms lurks in Big Tunnel, a tunnel between Fort Ritner and Tunnelton, Indiana. The tunnel, a 1,731-foot-long bore drilled in 1857, is located on the former B&O mainline to St. Louis. It curves through a rocky ridge deep in the White River Valley. A trip to the tunnel is a popular outing for Indiana teenagers, just like North Carolina's Maco Light once was for eastern North Carolina youths.

Above: Cowee Tunnel, near Dillsboro, North Carolina, when it was new.

Left: This former Southern Railway branch line crosses the Tuckasegee River and plunges into gloomy Cowee Tunnel, just west of Dillsboro, North Carolina. Now owned by the state and used by passenger and freight trains of the Great Smoky Mountains Railway, the tunnel has a history of spooky sights and sounds.

The most popular legend of Big Tunnel is that the ghost is a man, usually said to be a railroad watchman, who was murdered in the tunnel. Other stories say the man was killed by a train. In many of the stories, the murdered watchman is found hanging from a meat hook or spike at the center of the tunnel. Touching the spike or hook is said to bring bad luck.

The murdered watchman is said to appear as a misty form that makes low moans in the tunnel darkness. Others report seeing the gleam of an old kerosene lantern in the tunnel. More rarely, tunnel visitors report seeing a headless man signalling or walking with his head under his arm and a lantern in his hand. Some versions of the legend say the ghost is most often seen at midnight on rainy nights.

Older residents sometimes identify the ghost as Henry Dixon, a watchman said to have been murdered in the tunnel by local toughs during the early 1900's. The murder was a revenge killing, committed several days after Dixon stopped the toughs from raping a girl in the tunnel.

In the case of Big Tunnel, the historic facts are known and it is interesting to compare them with the legend. The tunnel was patrolled by a watchman from 1857 through 1908. The watchman walked through the tunnel after each train and removed any loose rock that fell from the walls or ceiling. After the tunnel was brick lined in 1908, the watchman was discharged. In fact, it was at about this time that a man named Henry Dixon was found murdered in the tunnel.

Other Big Tunnel legends tell of mass murders. One such legend is the story of the murdered convicts. Locals say that convicts were used to rebuild the tunnel at one time. They tried to escape, were all killed, and were buried in the tunnel floor. The legend says the humps of their graves may still be seen, and that the convicts' screams may be heard as you walk through the tunnel.

Other mass murder legends tell of Confederate soldiers or robbers being killed in or near the tunnel. Their ghosts are said to haunt the tunnel, too.

Teenagers who visit the tunnel also tell stories of recent murders. Usually the victim is said to have been a teenager who walked through the tunnel alone and was mysteriously murdered, perhaps by one of the tunnel haunts.

Few, if any, railroad sites are said to be haunted by as many ghosts as Big Tunnel.

East portal of Big Tunnel, 1990.

The Moonville Ghost

Southeastern Ohio is haunted by a trackside specter, the Moonville ghost. The story, as told by area resident Robin Lacy, goes like this:

> Many variations of the story float the night mists in the Raccoon Creek valley of Vinton County but they seem to agree on these points. The figure is tall—some say eight feet—and is a black man. He carries a brakeman's lantern glowing an eerie bluish light. He is seen in the area of Moonville, a name remaining from the late 19th century coal days, but today truly a ghost town without even palpable foundations for its store, post office and some 150 residences. But it did, indeed straddle the Marietta & Cincinnati Rail Road (as spelled on 1866 stock certificates) main line between Baltimore and St. Louis. In 1883 it became the B&O, and was abandoned by CSX in 1981.
>
> Immediately east of town stood the Moonville Tunnel, a shortish bore through a ridge of limestone, which sported a moss-encrusted brick portal on each end rather lovingly remodelled in the B&O tradition

by Chief Engineer J. M. Graham in 1903, according to a handsome bronze plaque just inside the east portal; quite similar in appearance to Big Tunnel. And it was inside this tunnel that a train struck and killed a local, off-duty brakeman one gloomy night as he attempted to flag it because of flood damage west of the tunnel toward Zaleski. Presumably buried in the extant graveyard on the ridge above the tunnel, the figure is said to be roaming the right-of-way still attempting to stop the train.

Now I speak from personal experience. The ridge and the tunnel bore unusual acoustic properties. One quiet, sunny afternoon in the late seventies, several members of my family were helping me discover this notable curiosity and had photographed the track, the portals, the plaque and the likely location of the non-existent town. We were walking west across the first steel girder bridge leaping Raccoon Creek when without warning of any kind a 70 car hot-shot west-bound freight exploded from the tunnel. There was no warning whistle and the first hint of the roar of the diesels came as we saw the "Chessie" on the front unit aimed straight at us.

We panicked, but scrambled for the mid-span refuge and covered our ears as three orange GPs side-swiped us and plunged down-grade leading a bizarrely un-ending assortment of freight cars toward Hamden, Chillicothe, then Cincinnati and points west at a good 40 mph. That experience was burned into my memory with such terrifying violence that whenever the Moonville ghost comes to mind my spine tingles with sympathy for his plight.

Variations of the story involve moonshine (copiously produced there-abouts), an innocent school teacher in white robes, and a laundry list of conflicting motives.

Alpine Tunnel

Alpine Tunnel is located on the abandoned, narrow-gauge Denver, South Park & Pacific near Pitkin, Colorado. Michael Woodill, who spent the night in the old telegrapher's shack near the bore in 1966, states that the tunnel is "spooky enough to make even this hard core skeptic believe." According to local legend, the tunnel is haunted by the ghost of an old engineer who was gassed in the tunnel when his train stalled.

The local legend is based on fact. In 1895, the tunnel was under reconstruction. A cave-in near the eastern entrance had blocked the flow of water out of the tunnel, and the dammed water was impeding the work. The Denver, South Park & Pacific superintendent, Mike Flavin, made the incredible decision of sending an engine into the tunnel to siphon out the water.

The danger involved soon became apparent: the tunnel workers began to be overcome by smoke. Work train conductor Elmer England led the workers out of the tunnel through the unblocked western portal, but one of them fell across the track. Before he could be retrieved, the rest of the train crew started backing the engine towards the western portal.

The engine was preceded by a worker with a torch, who found the man lying across the track. He reported this to the engineer, Dad Martenis, who reached for the throttle to shut off the steam and stop. At that moment, Martenis passed out, his weight fell on the throttle and the train plunged forwards towards the blocked eastern portal. It finally stopped when it hit the cave-in two hundred and fifty feet from the eastern entrance.

Conductor England made three attempts to reach the engine and run it back out to the west; he was finally overcome by the smoke and saved by one of the workers. Laborers finally reached the engine four hours later, when the fire in the locomotive died down.

The rescuers found a horrible sight. According to the "Gunnison Tribune" of June 14, 1895,

> Lying in the tender near the firebox was the body of Flavin, while on the engineer's side sat "Dad" Martenis, his head leaning out of the window, hand on the throttle. Fireman Byrnes had evidently fallen out of the cab, for he was found about ten feet behind the engine, in two feet of water, his face and head slightly bruised. These were the only scratches on any of the dead men. The engine had run into the rock and mud, and the pilot and headlight were broken. The bodies of Flavin and Martenis were warm, but Byrnes was stiff and cold. The men did everything they could to revive them, but all efforts proved futile.

While this tragedy was taking place inside the tunnel, a timbering crew was working just inside the east portal of the tunnel, on the

Diminutive 2-6-0 No. 71, built in 1884, pulled Denver, South Park & Pacific trains through the Colorado mountains.

other side of the cave-in from the trapped locomotive. One of the men, Oscar Cammann, had left his coat in the tunnel. Incredibly, he tried three times to retrieve it by crawling through a tiny, smoke-filled connecting hole at the apex of the cave-in. On his third, fatal attempt he was overcome by the fumes and became the fourth victim of the tragedy.

The Alpine Tunnel ghost legend perpetuates a folk memory of this accident, a strange and terrible mixture of stupidity and bravery.

Boardtree Tunnel

The Baltimore & Ohio's Boardtree Tunnel was plagued by misfortunes. Workers were killed in accidents and by trains; cholera swept the work camp and killed workers and their families. The many dead were buried in a cemetery on top of the tunnel.

One of the most popular workers on the job was Billy Hogan, an Irish section boss. He was a great character, witty, always playing

Ancient Denver, South Park & Pacific rail cars still sit near St. Elmo and Alpine Tunnel in Colorado; August 1972.

pranks. The unfortunate man was killed by the first train to pass through the tunnel after it was finished. He joined many of his co-workers in the cemetery above.

After the tunnel was finished, the trackwalker there was Packie Henderick. He had been a good friend of his fellow-countryman, Billy Hogan. Packie began to tell stories about Billy's ghost staying with him all day as he patrolled the tunnel.

Packie's job was affected by the ghost. When Billy was in a black mood, things went badly: bricks fell from the roof, tools were lost, a million little things went wrong. When Billy was in a good mood, though, he might even tell Packie where to look for faults in the rails or ties.

Other men began to think that Packie was a bit off. He'd tell them he was sharing his lunches with Billy and, sure enough, they'd find bits of food in the tunnel. It got to where the other workmen didn't want to walk through the tunnel at night. They would see a light at the tunnel opening that would vanish when they came up on it. Men began to whisper that the light was Billy Hogan's ghost.

Patrick E. Purcell

East portal of Alpine Tunnel, August 1972. Do the ghosts of the Alpine Tunnel work train crew haunt the scene of their tragic deaths?

After Packie died, though, the light stopped appearing and people forgot about Billy Hogan. It seems as if Packie's friendship was keeping Billy earthbound—that is until Packie finally joined him in the spirit world.

Grand Central Terminal, New York

New York City's Grand Central Terminal

Haunted Railroad Stations

*H*aunted railroad stations are not often found in American folklore. As mentioned above, this may be because railroad stations are rarely the scene of fatal mishaps and tragedy.

The Ghost of Grand Central

The Vanishing Samaritan is one railroad ghost that seems to be related to the vanishing hitchhiker legend. Another is the Ghost of Grand Central.

Back in the days when Grand Central was open twenty-four hours, the information clerk at the Golden Clock was approached by a very pretty girl of twenty or so. The clerk happened to notice it was 4:17 a.m.

The gateman and red cap saw the girl, too. She seemed lost and confused and embarrassed. She asked her way home, and gave an address just off Lexington Avenue in the upper Forties.

The red cap suggested a cab but the gateman, who was just getting off work, offered to walk the girl home. There was some quiet ribbing among the other men as the pair walked off.

The gateman and the girl walked up Lexington Avenue, the girl talking nervously about the aunt she lived with and about staying out late—how this was the first time she'd been out alone after eight. She talked about how angry her aunt would be.

They crossed the avenue and the girl quieted down. The gateman turned a corner and, when he looked over, he saw the girl wasn't with him any more. Frightened for her safety, he doubled back to Lexington, but she was nowhere in sight.

The girl had disappeared or given the gateman the slip. Worried because the girl had seemed so lost and confused, the gateman decided to search for her. He looked up and down Lex, peering into doorways. He found himself getting strangely agitated—the girl had made a weird impression on him.

After looking for her for some time, he decided to check at the address she'd given. He walked there and, even though it was still the wee hours, rang the bell. A frightened old woman answered. After the gateman told his story, the old woman sighed.

"She was my niece," the old woman said. "It happens this way every year. The poor girl was in the gas explosion when Grand Central was being built. She was taken to the hospital and died there a few hours later—it was thirty-eight years ago tonight."

The girl continued to appear on the anniversary of her death for many years. Today, Grand Central is only used by commuter trains—Amtrak's late-night runs use Penn Station. What does the poor lost girl do now?

Newark Central Station

Another big-city station haunting was the nineteenth century ghost train of Newark Central Station. One of the most amazing things about this phantom was its punctuality. Every midnight on the tenth day of almost every month during the entire decade of the 1870's, a ghost train was heard pulling into busy Newark Central Station.

No witness ever saw the train, but hundreds reported hearing a phantom whistle and the screech of flanges against iron rails as it ran through the station. On one memorable night, six hundred waiting passengers heard the ghostly train. It came to be known as the "Express Train to Hell."

The Ghost of Ransomville Station

Ransomville, a small town in upstate New York northeast of Niagara Falls, was located on the New York Central "Hojack" line that ran along Lake Ontario from Oswego to Niagara Falls.

The Ransomville station, now long abandoned, sits cold and desolate, the paint on its walls faded to a dirty white. Folks say that, on cold November nights, a bone-chilling scream can be heard from within the station. Old timers say the scream is the death agony of Hannah Scott.

Hannah Scott was killed at Ransomville station in 1863 by a Union Army troop train. Hannah and her husband Clarence were crossing the tracks in a buggy on a cold November night when the train hit them, dragging the buggy three hundred feet down the line.

Ransomville Historical Society, courtesy of Carlton Lisman

New York Central employees Fred Slocum (left) and Ellis Lisman (right) were photographed in the Ransomville, New York depot, December 1922. The ghost of a woman killed by a train near the station in 1863 is said to haunt the area.

Hannah was dragged with it, her screams only hushed when she was reduced to a crushed, bloody pulp by the train. The coroner carried her body into the station, beginning a haunting that's now over one hundred and thirty years old.

Local folks claim they hear Hannah's screams inside the station every November. Some even say they've seen a ghostly figure walking around the Ransomville depot.

Ghosts in the Waiting Room

Harpers Ferry, West Virginia might be America's most haunted community. It's not surprising, given the community's turbulent, tragic history, that it is the scene of a number of America's most famous hauntings.

The Harpers Ferry train station, still used by MARC commuter trains and Amtrak's "Capitol Limited," has been at the center of Harpers Ferry village life since the coming of the railroad. While the CSX, former Baltimore & Ohio, station no longer has an station agent/operator, it is still staffed by a ticket agent serving the MARC commuter trains.

For as long as railroad employees can remember, the station has been the scene of an unexplained phenomenon. Every once in a while, the station agent on duty has noticed noises in the waiting room when no one is there—noises as if a group of people was waiting for a train.

Then, the sound of a train headed by a long-vanished steam engine is heard. The train approaches, pulls into the station and stops. Then, the amazed employee on duty hears the people leave the waiting room, which falls silent. After that, the train pulls out of the station, fades into the distance, and all is quiet again until the next real, iron and steel train roars through Harpers Ferry.

Many an amazed agent, astounded by unexpected passengers and an unscheduled train, has burst into the waiting room or run to the trackside window, only to see…nothing.

No one knows why the Harpers Ferry station is haunted. Shirley Dougherty, a local historian who leads the famous Harpers Ferry ghost walks, has two theories as to why a ghost train frequents the Harpers Ferry station. The first is that the train may be connected

Caroline Weaver

Waiting room, Harpers Ferry, West Virginia ex-Baltimore & Ohio station at night.

with the John Brown raid on Harpers Ferry in 1859. Perhaps, Dougherty theorizes, the people haunting the waiting room were involved in the raid and they reenact the time they spent waiting for their horrible rendezvous with history.

Dougherty's second theory is that the haunting is a reenactment of a nineteenth century tragedy. According to local legend, when the first regular train came though Harpers Ferry during construction of the Baltimore & Ohio, a woman wearing one of the period's hoop skirts was sucked underneath the wheels of the train and killed. Perhaps she is repeating her appointment with death over and over through eternity.

Eby Witzke Returns

The former Great Northern branch through New London, Minnesota is now abandoned, and the old station in downtown New London has been converted to a residence. It is said to be haunted by the friendly ghost of former agent Eby Witzke, who died while working in the building in about 1900. He has only appeared a few times in the intervening years.

Denver Union Station

Denver, Colorado's impressive Union Station, still used by Amtrak, is reportedly haunted by a man nicknamed "Soldier" by station employees. People do not so much see the ghost as sense his presence: a military officer lurking in the great hall of the station. Perhaps "Soldier" is a World War I or II casualty who left for war from Denver, never to return.

The ghost might or might not be the same phantom as was reported in Denver Union Station during the 1930's. A shadowy apparition which seemed to be trying to find its way out of the station appeared several times during the '30s. It eventually vanished, putting an end to Union Station hauntings until "Soldier" showed up.

According to legend, one of the old Denver depots was so haunted that it was torn down. The station, which was located on 22nd Street in downtown Denver, was haunted by a number of phantoms who were frequently seen by operators and agents working in the building.

The most terrifying of these was the ghost of a three-fingered tramp. The phantom hobo frightened ticket agents by tapping on ticket windows, and was seen dozens of times over a decade of appearances. He always appeared at two a.m., and also haunted train platforms, the station lobby, and station offices.

Salt Lake City Depot Ghosts

Both ends of the old Denver & Rio Grande Western are haunted: the Denver Union Station and the Denver & Rio Grande Western Salt Lake City depot. The D&RGW depot in Salt Lake City, built in about 1910, houses the Utah State Historical Society and is still the Salt Lake City Amtrak stop.

Like the station in Denver, the Salt Lake City depot is reportedly haunted by a number of phantoms. People have talked about presences in the building since the World War II years. The ghost most often seen is a black-haired woman wearing a purple dress. According to legend, her life was crushed out on one of the station tracks when she dived in front of a train trying to save her engagement ring, which her faithless fiancee had thrown onto the right-of-

Denver, Colorado's much-haunted Union Station.

The Denver & Rio Grande Western station in Salt Lake City, Utah.

way. She haunts the ladies room in the station and the Rio Grande Cafe.

According to a building custodian, ghosts also haunt the basement of the building. The worker claims to have interrupted an entire party of spooks down there one night.

The last D&RGW depot ghost is an invisible presence that is more felt than seen. It has given a bad case of the shivers to historical society employees and building security guards in the lobby and on the station's balcony during the wee hours.

Northern Pacific Depot and Adjoining Park, Livingston, Mont.

Livingston, Montana,(top) and Glendive, Montana (bottom) stations on the old Northern Pacific main line haunted by the ghost of Glendive.

N. P. Depot, Glendive, Mont.

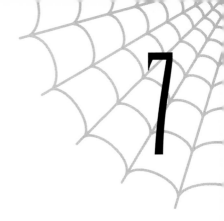

Haunts in the Rail Cars

*H*aunted rail cars are almost as rare as haunted railroad stations. As already mentioned, it seems likely that the reason for our shortage of haunted rail cars is transience: the fact that people rarely encounter the same rail car a second time, and often wouldn't know it even if they did.

It is interesting to note that two of the phantoms mentioned below haunt passengers on a certain train or trains running on a certain route, regardless of the cars making up the trains. In these cases, the general public has had a chance to build up a legend about a specific, regularly scheduled train or a certain route—something with continuity.

Similarly, the haunted business cars reported below are vehicles with long histories that people—often the same people--return to over and over again. This gives ghost legends associated with particular cars a chance to develop.

On the other hand, the haunted engines and haunted caboose mentioned below were reported by railroad men—the only people with the opportunity to ride the same caboose or engine with great regularity. Again, we see the factor of continuity of experience, of familiarity, that seems to be so important in the creation of ghost lore.

Finally, it should be noted that old time railroaders had many superstitions about rolling stock and locomotives, especially about "hoodooed engines" and the like. Their common superstitions about engines are described below; there were many others, such as a taboo against turning engines against the sun on a turntable. Since these beliefs take us far out of the realm of railroad ghost folklore, I've not gone any farther into them here. B. A. Botkin and Alvin F. Harlow discuss them at greater length in their classic work, "A Treasury of Railroad Folklore."

Haunted "Tamalpais"

"Tamalpais", an ex-Atchison, Topeka & Santa Fe Railway business car, is reportedly haunted by an unseen phantom. People who've been in the car often report feeling that someone else is in it when no one is actually there.

One rider was in the "Tamalpais" lounge at night when he felt the presence of another person. In a dark railroad car at night, the windows reflect the interior of the car. When the rider felt a presence in the car, he turned. He saw a shadow cross the window, but by the time he had turned all the way around no one was there.

More concrete—and annoying—are the moving tools. Maintenance people working on "Tamalpais" have frequently reported that their tools have been moved around the car overnight. Tools have also been rearranged while workers are taking a break.

People familiar with the car feel it is haunted by the ghost of Ray Adams, once executive vice president and assistant general manager of Western Lines for the Santa Fe. He was the last railroad officer to use the car and he made sure that it wasn't scrapped.

Chicago & North Western business car 400

Perhaps the most famous haunted railroad car is Chicago & North Western's business car 400. The car is said to be haunted by former Chicago & North Western President Jim Wolfe.

The car was built by Pullman for the New York Central in 1928, and was later sold to the West India Fruit & Steamship Company. The car was purchased by the C&NW in 1980 and was completely remodeled in 1981. Renumbered 400, it was assigned to C&NW President Jim Wolfe.

President Wolfe was an enthusiastic proponent of the railroad's business car fleet, and 400 was used by him on many trips to Wyoming's Powder River Basin coal area. The car was often used by the railroad president as he courted potential shippers.

Although Wolfe was an adamant opponent of passenger trains, he grew very attached to his private car. His feeling for the car was so strong that he reportedly was insulted when another executive refused to use the 400 for a business trip.

Wolfe died of cancer at the age of 58 on August 9, 1988. Just days after his death, C&NW employees began to report strange happenings in car 400. The railroad company's official explanation for these incidents is practical jokes played by car workers.

Many C&NW employees believe, however, that Wolfe's concern for car 400 is transcending the man's death. Workers report toilets that flush by themselves, call bells that ring themselves, and untraceable rattles and vibrations throughout the car. The car is also prone to sudden temperature drops. C&NW employees have apparently accepted the phenomena at face value, however, and do not seem reluctant to work on the car.

The most amazing incident in the car 400 haunting involves the chef who often served Wolfe aboard the car. The chef, who retired in 1990, reported that he was cooking steaks in a car two cars ahead of the 400 one night soon after Wolfe's death. Two other riders were in the car just ahead of the 400.

According to them, the 400's door opened and a man walked through the car towards the chef's car. With a shock, one of the riders recognized the passerby as Wolfe. Wolfe then went to the chef's kitchen in the next car. At first, the chef just felt Wolfe's presence, but then he could see the ghost.

Wolfe, the chef reported, was wearing a shirt and jacket that matched C&NW's corporate colors of yellow and green—the way he often dressed on inspection trips. He appeared relaxed, and said, "George, I'm hungry!" several times.

The chef asked Wolfe to step into another car so he could cook him a dinner. He then ran to the car behind where he found his co-workers, who were still shaken by Wolfe's reappearance. A deeply religious man, the chef felt he should do as the ghost had asked, so he returned to his kitchen and laid a full meal out for Wolfe.

Another time, the chef was awakened by Wolfe's voice saying, "Get up, there's something wrong." The chef ran through the train until he found an empty car that smelled of smoke. He then heard Wolfe's voice saying, "Smother it, George." The chef then shut down the car's air conditioning equipment, sealed the doors and called a technician. He had caught the fire just in time.

From that time until the chef's retirement, he always asked for the 400 to be assigned to any trip he was working. And, whenever he worked on a trip that included the 400, he always set out a full dinner for Jim Wolfe.

Haunted Nevada Railcars

Nevada ghost lore is responsible for two stories of haunted railcars. One is the legend of Southern Pacific express car No.5. Apparently, the railroad lost a body being shipped back east aboard the car in 1881. After that, Wells Fargo men working on car No.5 were frequently visited by an angry phantom shouting, "What was done with the corpse?"

Another haunted Nevada railcar was a dining car owned by the Nevada-California-Oregon Railway. The ghost of a Chinese cook murdered aboard the car haunted it so regularly that the diner was finally scrapped.

The Haunted Caboose

Years ago, a conductor named Runyon, who worked the Wabash Railway's run between Kansas City and Moberly, Missouri, was killed in his caboose when his train wrecked.

The caboose was rebuilt and assigned to the new conductor on the same run. After several years, this conductor, whose name was John Enzline, was assigned a new engineer named Snyder.

After the new engineer's first Kansas City-Moberly run was finished and the train was tied up, the crew went to the railroad beanery for dinner. Enzline complained over corned beef, cabbage, and coffee that his caboose was haunted by Runyon's ghost.

"That's baloney," said Snyder. "There's no such thing as ghosts."

"O.K., pard," said Enzline. "I'll tell you what. I'll stay in the caboose tonight if you will."

So Snyder and Enzline agreed to spend the night together in the haunted caboose. They walked out to the caboose track and piled into the caboose's bunks.

Snyder was just dozing off when he heard a groan and a shriek.

"Alright, John," he yelled, "cut that out."

"I'm not doing nothin'," Enzline yelled back.

Even as Enzline spoke, groans resounded through the little caboose again. Snyder, still convinced there must be an explanation for all this, searched the hack from top to bottom, then looked around for anything outside that might be making the sounds.

"It's no use," Enzline said. "I've checked her a hundred times, and never could find anything that'd make a noise like that!"

Snyder, who was pretty worried now, went back to bed. After awhile, the groans started up again and kept going for what seemed like an eternity. Finally, Snyder gave in, and both men went up to the railroad rooming house so they could get some sleep.

Wabash crews complained about the caboose so much over the years that it was finally scrapped.

Ghost of the "Flying Yankee"

During the 1890s, a train known as "The Flying Yankee" ran from New York to Miami. Once, a young man was riding the train on the way to marry his Southern sweetheart. As the train raced through North Carolina, the man slipped while passing between the coaches, fell, and was crushed beneath the wheels of the train. He never saw his lover again.

Soon afterwards, passengers on "The Flying Yankee" began to report sightings of an apparition on the train, a sad man standing in dark corners. In the folklore of the times, the ghost was believed to be that of the unfortunate young lover killed by the train.

For many years, the ghostly lover was seen, seeking in vain to reach his sweetheart at the end of "The Flying Yankee's" run.

The Ghost of Glendive

The state of Montana has been the scene of big-time railroading since the late years of the nineteenth century. In recent years, all of the passenger trains through Montana have used the former Great Northern route through Glacier National Park and Havre.

Until just a few years ago, though, passenger trains also ran on the old Northern Pacific route. Westbound, this line passes through Wibaux, Glendive, Miles City, and on to Billings and Butte. This route, now bereft of passenger trains, was said to be haunted by the Dead Man of Glendive.

According to local folklore, the Glendive ghost was that of a man killed in a train on its way to Miles City. Afterwards, his ghost haunted passenger trains on the route. The Dead Man of Glendive's ghost was an agonized phantom that appeared to want something from those who saw it. Locals believe that the man was looking for someone who could release him from his incessant riding of the trains.

Maybe, now that no passenger trains tread the old N. P. between Miles City and Glendive, the Dead Man can rest easy. Was that what he needed to release him from his haunting doom?

Locomotive 49

Until recently, locomotive 49 was part of the Rail City Museum in Sandy Pond, New York. The museum had sixteen locomotives and fifty cars. 49, which was built in about 1920, was part of a group of several similar locomotives. All were 0-4-0 saddletankers built by Alco, a locomotive works once located in Schenectady, New York.

49 was originally built for the Solvay Process Company's Jamesville Quarry. The quarry operated a stone crusher, which is still located at the old quarry site.

Engine 49 was used to bring stone to the crusher, which was built high on the side of a hill. The tracks that led to the crusher ran through the side of the building. Once in the building, the side-dump cars used in the train dropped rock into the crusher, which reduced the stone from boulders as large as five feet in diameter to five-inch gravel. The track continued out of the building and terminated on a stub-end trestle. As the locomotive at the front of the train unloaded car after car, it got closer and closer to the end of the trestle.

Locomotive 49 was a bad luck engine, called "The Ghost" by its crews. Its first mishap was when it had a cut of the side-dump cars one night in 1947, and was dumping rock into the crusher. It was about eight p.m. The engineer fell asleep and the locomotive ran right off the end of the trestle and one hundred feet into the crusher building. The engineer didn't ride the engine all the way down to his death—he managed to jump and save himself.

Locomotive 49 ended up embedded in the fifth floor of the

crusher building, causing $100,000 in damage. It was removed from the building in sections and sent to Alco, where it was rebuilt with a new boiler and water tank.

49 was returned to the Jamesville Quarry in about 1950. Then came the second, fatal mishap. It was one evening soon after the engine's return from the Alco plant, again at about eight p. m. The engine was sitting on a track with steam up. It was hit by another engine, and 49's engineer was scalded to death by a broken steam pipe.

After that horrible accident, if the locomotive was ever under steam at the eight o'clock hour, it would give off a smell of burning flesh. The men at the quarry also claimed that every once in a while the engine's bell would ring itself and its whistle would blow as if the cord was pulled by a ghostly hand. This eerie manifestation always happened at eight p. m. as well. Naturally, engineers who worked at the Jamesville Quarry began to avoid working on engine 49.

Steam operations at the Jamesville Quarry ended in 1953, and 49 was bought by Rail City at auction in 1954. From the mid-fifties through the mid-seventies, 49 was a display engine at Rail City and was never fired up. The engine's ghost story was told as part of the Rail City train ride.

The engine was recently sold and the new owner, who lives in Pennsylvania, is restoring and reactivating locomotive 49. Will the ghost of the scalded engineer be awakened again after resting in peace for over forty years?

Hoodoo Engines

In this collection of tales, we've met ghost trains, ghosts who lurk along the track, ghostly lights, and a haunted caboose. We'll end off not with a specific haunted place or a specific ghost, but with a general superstition that railroaders have.

Railroad workers, especially during the age of steam, believed that certain engines were unlucky or "hoodooed." When an engine is hoodooed, it is involved in many more mishaps than the average engine. In the worst cases, it becomes a man-killer and racks up a number of fatal wrecks.

That this superstition has some basis in fact is indisputable. Certain engines in railroad history have been involved in more wrecks than other engines on the same railroad, even engines of a similar class. Whether the reason for this is mechanical, supernatural, or a freak of statistics, it is hard to say.

Even more interesting is the connection old railroad men made between engine numbers and the hoodoo spell. The numbers nine and thirteen were especially feared by old-time railroad men, who delighted in telling stories about the gruesome exploits of "old number nine" on such and such a railroad. Even multiples of nine, or engine numbers containing nine, were frequently looked upon with a jaundiced eye.

One exception to the "nine or thirteen" theory was Casey Jones's infamous ten-wheeler, No. 382, which was rebuilt after his famous, fatal accident but was long considered a hoodoo engine on the

The "Casey Jones engine," Illinois Central Railroad No. 382, Water Valley, Mississippi, October 1900.

Illinois Central. It was retired in 1935 after causing several more deaths, including that of the fireman on her last run, who was killed when she jumped the tracks on her way to the scrap yard.

Another jinxed engine was locomotive No. 571 of the Northern Pacific Railroad, known to NP railroaders as "Hoodoo." The locomotive, which was based in Fargo, North Dakota at the turn of the century, was eventually involved in three wrecks that killed a num-

Denver & Rio Grande narrow-gauge No. 108, an American type (4-4-0) built in 1883, was a sister to "Dread 107."

ber of railroad men.

The locomotive's deadly career of mishaps started when it derailed in 1892 and plunged into the Green River. The most interesting aspect of the No. 571 legend is the hideous goblin that began appearing, perched on the locomotive's pilot, to engineers after the Green River wreck.

Perhaps the most jinxed engine of all, though, was Denver & Rio Grande narrow gauge Number 107, an American type built in 1883. If ever an engine was piloted by the angel of death, it was this one. D&RG employees swore the steamer was haunted by the wraiths of the fourteen railroaders killed aboard her.

The engine's reign of terror started with a bridge washout in Black Eagle Canyon, an accident that killed the engineer and fireman. 107 lay in the canyon until the river level dropped in late summer, when she was raised and repaired.

The 107's next engineer, Bill Godfrey, was killed along with his fireman and several passengers when the steamer struck a ten-ton boulder at a spot near Gunnison, Colorado known as Blind Man's Curve. It was at about this time that men began to believe there was something wrong with the engine. She acquired the nickname "Dread 107," and folks began to say that demons and ghosts haunted her cab at night as she stood silent in the roundhouse.

After the two wrecks, the engine was transferred to the Salt Lake

City-to-Ogden run, a safer ride through prairie country. For a number of years, Dread 107's trips were uneventful by railroading standards of the era, resulting in a few minor collisions and the death of a hobo who was riding the back of 107's tender when the steamer derailed.

When engineer Ole Gleason was assigned 107, though, the curse came back with a vengeance. After six months at the engine's throttle, he and four other railroaders were killed in a head-on collision. After this tragedy, a D&RG worker carved the 107's record in the woodwork of the engine's cab, including a list of her wrecks and the names of all the men who had died aboard her. This ghoulish record, the railroad equivalent of notches in a bad man's gun, seemed to defuse Dread 107's curse for a while; although her crews and their families seemed to be dogged by general bad luck.

Finally, though, tragedy struck her again in a most weird and gruesome way. At the time, the engine ran out of Ogden Yard and was crewed by the Flynn brothers, with Tom Flynn at the throttle. One day, Tom was making a run with his brother when he started to brood over the death list carved into the cab wall. In a sudden fit of insanity, he attacked his own brother, threw him from the speeding cab, and then let the engine run away. She overturned after a mad run down the track, pinning Tom, now a raving maniac, under her. Tom's brother died from his injuries.

The engine had such a bad name now that Salt Lake City-Ogden crews wouldn't work on her. D&RG management transferred her to Alamosa, where she was given a major overhaul, the death list was erased from her cab wall, and she was renumbered 100.

In most cases, renumbering a hoodoo engine breaks the fatal spell. Not so with Dread 107, now D&RG 100. Several years later, she went in the ditch, apparent victim of a spring washout. She returned to Alamosa for repairs and, for some reason, her old number was restored!

Dread 107 soon took ample advantage of her renewed hoodoo. One June evening, engineer Frank Murphy was at the throttle as 107 headed a gravel train downgrade from Mear's Junction to Alamosa. The train ran away and smashed into a light mixed train. No one will ever know what caused the runaway as the gravel train's entire crew, five men, was killed.

After 107 eliminated five more railroaders, D&RG employees simply refused to work aboard or behind her. She was scrapped in 1908 after a twenty-five-year career of death and destruction.

Residents of Grand Junction, Colorado claim that even scrapping could not end Dread 107's reign of terror. Since she was broken up, her ghost has been seen running down the ex-Denver & Rio Grande Western outside of Grand Junction. She is most often seen where the track runs along the Gunnison River between Grand Junction and Montrose. Sometimes witnesses hear her whistle but never actually see the cursed engine.

Death leaned out from the cab window, piloting 107 the night she piled up on Blind Man's Curve.

Afterword

Ghost trains and train wrecks; haunted tracks, tunnels, stations, and trains—such are the stuff of which America's ghostly railroad legends are made. The sweep of railroad ghost folklore is amazing. The stories recorded in this book surely only scratch the surface of the mass of ghostly train legends haunting America and waiting to be recorded. Many of them are already forgotten, or soon will be, swept away in the asphalt-covered path of today's transitory American lifestyle.

Where do the stories come from? Melissa Ellis, until recently director of North Carolina's Wilmington Railroad Museum, got a lot of questions about the Maco Light, the famous railroad ghost that appeared just a few miles away. She has a theory about railroad ghosts, a theory based on the characteristics of old-time railroad men.

"Railroaders are an interesting group," Ellis says, "superstitious, close-knit, full of stories. They come up with legends like the Maco Light to explain things that can't be explained."

Wherever they come from, railroad ghost legends are an important part of American ghost lore. They are also entertaining reminders of days gone by.

Notes on the Sources

Lincoln's Train   Lincoln's ghost train, which is also sometimes reported on the Harlem Division of the old New York Central, has a basis in fact. The famous funeral train which carried Abraham Lincoln's body from Washington, D.C. to Springfield, Illinois looked a lot like the ghost train of legend. The train really did pass over the Hudson River Railroad, later the Hudson Division of the old New York Central, from New York to Albany in April, 1865.

The story has been reported in a number of sources, most notably Lloyd Lewis's "Myths After Lincoln" (New York: Harcourt, Brace and Company, 1929), p. 395, and Louis C. Jones's "Things That Go Bump in the Night" (Syracuse, New York: Syracuse University Press, 1983), pp. 154-155. Many other versions have been adapted from the accounts in these two books. Lewis originally found the story in an Albany newspaper.

The Warsaw Ghost Train   A fuller account of the Warsaw ghost train may be found in Nancy Roberts' "North Carolina Ghosts and Legends" (Columbia, South Carolina: University of South Carolina Press, 1991), pp. 60-64.

The Catsburg Ghost Train Catsburg Store is located on Old Oxford Road just northeast of the Braggtown section of Durham, North Carolina. Phil Petty is a regular at the store, which is run by Polly and Harvey Wensel. Collected from Petty in December 1991 by Anthony W. Reevy. Informant and store owners obviously did not believe the story, and saw it as an amusing local legend. See also Ann Green, "The phantom train of Catsburg" in "Durham Herald-Sun", October 31, 1991, pp. A8-A9.

According to Glenn E. Taylor, writing in the January/February 1995 Norfolk Southern "Paces", p. 17, an accident did occur at Catsburg Store in 1940. A high school student named Ritchie and his grandmother were killed by a train at the grade crossing there; the boy's two sisters survived.

According to Taylor, the Catsburg Store was named for its owner, Durham County sheriff Cat Blevins, who was famed for his stealth in tracking down criminals —hence the nickname "Cat." Cat Blevins gave his nickname to the store and, later, this Durham County neighborhood.

Ghost Train of Dalton, Georgia "Phantom Train." "Railroad Magazine", June 1954, p. 119. "Railroad Magazine" states the story originally appeared in "The Citizen" (Dalton, Georgia), and then in the "Railroad Gazette" of January, 1881.

The Ghost Train of Nineveh Junction From the Utica & Mohawk Valley Chapter, National Railway Historical Society newsletter, "Tower Topics", June 1994, page 9, taken from Chenango County Historian's "Newsletter" No.16 (Spring/Summer 1994), transcribed by the Oneida County Historical Society. "Tower Topics" editorial note: "Doug Preston gave us this story which was authored by chapter member Doug Ellison, who is the CEO of the Adirondack Scenic Railroad."

Author Ellison notes: "This story was probably related to me ten or fifteen years ago, ca. 1978, and briefly made the rounds of rail enthusiasts frequenting the Binghamton-Oneonta areas. The identity of the driver was always concealed, as it was said he was a man of very respectable character who wished to remain that way." (Author's note dated August 25, 1992).

Many thanks to Doug Ellison for permission to reproduce his story about the ghost train of Nineveh Junction.

Yazoo & Mississippi Valley Ghost Train Folklorist Richard M. Dorson recounted the story of the Y&MV ghost train in his "Negro Folktales in Michigan" (Cambridge, Massachusetts: Harvard University Press, 1956), pp. 126-127.

Ghost Train of Gaskins, Arkansas From "an old issue of "Railroad Magazine"" quoted in James R. Fair, Jr., "The North Arkansas Line" (San Diego: Howell-North Books, 1969), p. 100. According to Richard and Judy Dockrey Young in "Ozark Ghost Stories" (Little Rock, Arkansas: August House Publishers, Inc., 1995), p. 74, a ghost caboose rolled down the old Missouri & North Arkansas right-of-way after the trains stopped running but before the tracks were taken up.

The Ghost Train of the Arizona Desert More details about the Ghost Train of the Arizona Desert may be found in Jean Anderson's "The Haunting of America: Ghost Stories from Our Past" (Boston: Houghton Mifflin Company, 1973), pp. 150-155, and Betty Baker, ed., "Great Ghost Stories of the Old West" (New York: Four Winds Press, 1968), pp. 99-110.

Another improbable railroad ghost legend of Arizona concerns ghost camels seen from trains. The camels must be a folk memory of the unsuccessful nineteenth century experiment with camels by the U. S. Army.

Belleville, Texas's Phantom Train See Dennis William Hauck, "The National Directory of Haunted Places", p. 337; and Brad Steiger and Sherry Hansen-Steiger, Montezuma's Serpent And Other True Supernatural Tales of the Southwest"

(New York: Paragon House, 1992), p. 39.

Ghost Train of Mayer, Arizona   Richard Allen Young and Judy Dockrey Young, "Ghost Stories from the American Southwest" (Little Rock, Arkansas: August House Publishers, 1991), pp. 126-127, 181.

Ghost Train of Marshall Pass   B. A. Botkin, ed., "A Treasury of American Folklore" (New York: Crown Publishers, 1944), pp. 714-715, from Charles M. Skinner, "Myths and Legends of Our Own Land" (Philadelphia and London: J. B. Lippincott Company, 1896), Vol. II, pp. 192-195.

Kansas Pacific Ghost Train   S. J. Sackett and William E. Koch, eds., "Kansas Folklore" (Lincoln, Nebraska: University of Nebraska Press, 1961), pp. 42-43.

Retribution: A Mystery Story of White's Hill   Chas. Cleveland. "Retribution: A Mystery Story of White's Hill." "Headlight", October, 1986, pp. 2-4. Originally published in Northwestern Pacific's "Headlight", 1928.

The Phantom Locomotive, Number 110   From Thomas W. Dixon, Jr., "The Rise and Fall of Alderson, West Virginia" (Parsons, West Virginia: McClain Printing Company, 1967), pp. 125-127. Reprinted with permission of the author.

Ghost of the White Train   Richard Peyton, ed., "Journey Into Fear" (New York: Wings Books, 1991), p. 51.

Pittsfield, Massachusetts Ghost Train   Dennis William Hauck, "The National Directory of Haunted Places", p. 191; and Richard Williams, "Quest for the Unknown: Bizarre Phenomena" (Pleasantville, New York: Reader's Digest, 1992).

Phantom Locomotive of Stevens Point   Richard Peyton, "Journey Into Fear", p. 72.

The Statesville Ghost Train   A full account of the Statesville ghost train may be found in Bruce and Nancy Roberts' "This Haunted Land" (Charlotte, North Carolina: McNally and Loftin, Publishers, 1970), pp. 9-13. The wreck really did happen as described here.

Bill Hoke, now of Charlotte, described the local folklore concerning the Bostian's Bridge area in a telephone interview on July 15, 1994. The author visited the wreck site during the early morning hours of August 27, 1991.

Another ghost train legend told by storytellers in the North Carolina foothills concerns the old Southern Railway branch from Chester, South Carolina through Gastonia, Lincolnton, Newton, Hickory, and Lenoir, North Carolina. The author has been unable to find details about this most elusive of American railroad ghost legends.

The Ghost Wreck of Zoar Valley   Catherine Harris Ainsworth, "Legends of New York State" (Buffalo, New York: Catherine Harris Ainsworth, 1978), p. 93.

The Phantom Wreck of Rowlesburg   Ruth Ann Musick, "The Telltale Lilac Bush and Other West Virginia Ghost Tales" (Lexington, Kentucky: University of Kentucky Press, 1965), p. 125.

McDonough, Georgia Ghost Train   See Ronald G. Killion and Charles T. Waller, "A Treasury of Georgia Folklore" (Atlanta: Cherokee Publishing Company, 1972), p. 54.

The Headless Brakeman   A version of the headless brakeman story may be found in Things That Go Bump in the Night", a book about New York State ghosts by Louis C. Jones, pp. 52-54.

The Headless Ghost at Free Springs Bridge   Ronald L. Baker, "Hoosier Folk Legends" (Bloomington, Indiana: Indiana University Press, 1982), pp. 68-69.

The Headless Trainman of Fairmont   Ruth Ann Musick, "The Telltale Lilac Bush and Other West Virginia Ghost Tales", p. 124.

The Body Under the Train   Ruth Ann Musick, "The Telltale Lilac Bush and Other West Virginia Ghost Tales", p. 121.

The Maco Light   The Maco Light is one of America's most famous ghost stories, and is certainly our most famous railroad ghost. The Atlantic Coast Line included the story in a promotional pamphlet, and it has since found its way into popular works such as Ben Botkin and Alvin Harlow's "A Treasury of Railroad Folklore" (New York: Crown Publishers, 1953), pp. 398-399; John Harden's "Tar Heel Ghosts" (Chapel Hill, North Carolina: The University of North Carolina Press, 1954), pp. 44-51; and Richard Walser's "North Carolina Legends" (Raleigh, North Carolina: North Carolina Division of Archives and History, 1980), pp. 50-52. Famous ghost hunter Hans Holzer spent a great deal of time investigating the Maco Light, and it is featured at length in several of his books, most notably "The Phantoms of Dixie" (Indianapolis and New York: The Bobbs-Merrill Company, Inc., 1972), pp. 68-90.

The Phantom Stationmaster Tucker R. Littleton. "Ghosts and Haunted Houses of Eastern North Carolina." "North Carolina Folklore" VIII, No. 1 (July 1960): pp. 24-25. The story was collected by Miss Patsy Whitehurst, Beaufort High School senior, 1958-59.

The Mintz Ghost Light- The Vander Ghost Light Detailed in "Swamp gas? Apparition? Lights remain a mystery," an Associated Press story by Larry Bingham that appeared in the "Durham Herald-Sun", December 26, 1993, pp. G1 and G5. See also John Hairr, "Bizarre Tales of the Cape Fear Country" (Fuquay-Varina, North Carolina: Triangle Books, 1995), pp. 60-63.

The Cohoke Ghost Light Robert Reisweber, letter, Williamsburg, Virginia, May 23, 1994. Also, L. B. Taylor, Jr. "The Ghosts of Tidewater ...and nearby environs" (Williamsburg, Virginia: L. B. Taylor, Jr., 1990), pp. 50-54.

The Suffolk Ghost Light L. B. Taylor, Jr. "The Ghosts of Tidewater...and nearby environs", pp. 54-55.

The Hookerman Henry Jewell, telephone interview, Great Meadows, New Jersey, June 27, 1994. Detail about the origin of the name "Hookerman" from David Delaney, Internet posting, Boston, June 25, 1994.

The Headless Engineer's Light W. K. McNeil, ed., "Ghost Stories from the American South" (New York: Dell Publishing Co., 1985), p. 15. See also Dennis William Hauck, "The National Directory of Haunted Places", p. 326-327; and Kathryn Tucker Windham, "Thirteen Tennessee Ghosts & Jeffrey" (University of Alabama Press, 1987). The light is seen along the tracks near an unpaved road that dips to cross the former L&N west of the town of Chapel Hill. Witnesses usually face north along the tracks as the light approaches.

The Senath Ghost Light John L. Yarbro, Internet posting, June 16, 1994.

The Crossett, Arkansas Ghost Light See Richard Alan Young and Judy Dockrey Young, "Ghost Stories from the American Southwest" (Little Rock, Arkansas: August House Publishers, 1991), pp. 41-42, 167. Crossett, Arkansas was a rail junction served by the Arkansas & Louisiana Missouri, the Missouri Pacific, the Ashley, Drew & Northern, and the Chicago, Rock Island & Pacific. A similar light with a similar legend attached to it is said to appear along the tracks at nearby Gurdon, Arkansas, a junction on the old Missouri Pacific.

The Concord Ghost Light The author learned of the Concord ghost light from Mrs. Emily J. Patterson of Greensboro, North Carolina, granddaughter of Alexander Campbell. Information on Campbell's death and the subsequent reports of a haunting come from the "Concord Times" of December 14, 1888, the "Concord Standard Weekly" of December 14, 1888 and an unidentified newspaper clipping provided by Mrs. Patterson.

Johnny Marsden's Light Freeman Hubbard, "Superstitions", "Railroad Magazine", April 1949, pp. 50-51.

Red Light for Danger See Michael Norman and Beth Scott, "Historic Haunted America" (New York: Tom Doherty Associates, 1995), p. 219. Carlin, Nevada is also the site of a Nevada railroad haunting: a conductor killed in an accident often returned to the railroad yards there.

The Big Thicket Ghost Light From Richard Alan Young and Judy Dockrey

Young, "Ghost Stories from the American Southwest", pp. 47-48. See also Joan Bingham and Dolores Riccio, "More Haunted Houses" (New York: Pocket Books, 1991), pp. 61-65.

Glowing Eyes on the Track W. K. McNeil, "Ghost Stories from the American South", pp. 88-89, 181-182.

Another curious phantom that appears occasionally along America's railroads is the ghost, usually friendly, of a large white dog. This legend, which seems to originate in Texas, is mentioned in J. Mason Brewer, "Dog Ghosts and Other Texas Negro Folk Tales" (Austin: University of Texas Press, 1958), pp. 89-92.

Railroad Bill Morris Slater, a.k.a. Railroad Bill, really lived. He was a bandit who robbed stores and freight trains. Apparently, he was driven to a life of crime by being mistakenly identified as a boxcar thief by railroad detectives. After a long hunt, which lasted from 1894 until 1897, Bill was finally shot and killed by a rural Alabama storekeeper. Along the way, Bill robbed many boxcars, killed a number of lawmen, and eluded capture by a succession of Louisville & Nashville railroad policemen and Alabama sheriffs. His long success in eluding capture despite the formidable odds against him made Railroad Bill an folk hero among Alabama African-Americans.

His legend is less well-known today, but a song about him, "Railroad Bill," is a very popular American blues ballad. Norm Cohen's "Long Steel Rail: The Railroad in American Folksong" (Urbana, Illinois: University of Illinois Press, 1981), pp. 122-131, contains a good discussion of Railroad Bill's place in legend and song. The ghost legend is from Nancy and Bruce Roberts' "This Haunted Land", pp. 65-67.

Flag Stop See Dennis William Hauck, "The National Directory of Haunted Places", p. 204; and Kathryn Tucker Windham, "Thirteen Mississippi Ghosts & Jeffrey" (University of Alabama Press, 1987).

The Railroader's Return Louis C. Jones, "Things That Go Bump in the Night", p. 48; Patrick W. Gainer, "Witches, Ghosts and Signs: Folklore of the Southern Appalachians" (Grantsville, West Virginia: Seneca Books, 1975), pp. 84-85; and Freeman Hubbard, "Superstitions", p. 53.

Ghostly Music The story of the ghostly music was first reported by West Virginia folklorist Ruth Ann Musick in her "Coffin Hollow and Other Ghost Tales", pp. 29-30.

Screaming Jenny Shirley Dougherty, telephone interview, Harpers Ferry, West Virginia, June 23, 1994.

Dead Man in a Derby Hat Dennis William Hauck, "The National Directory of Haunted Places", p. 87. Also MaryJoy Martin, "Twilight Dwellers: Ghosts, Ghouls & Goblins of Colorado" (Boulder, Colorado: Pruett Publishing, 1985).

Ghost of Mud Cut Eliot Wigginton, editor, "Foxfire 2" (Garden City, New York: Anchor Books, 1973), pp. 346-347.

A Ghostly Race More about the ghostly horse and rider may be found in James Reynolds' "Ghosts in American Houses" (New York: Bonanza Books, 1955), pp. 183-184.

The Ghostly Confederate From Freeman Hubbard, "Superstitions", p. 48. See also Ronald G. Killion and Charles T. Waller, "A Treasury of Georgia Folklore" (Atlanta: Cherokee Publishing Company, 1972), p. 53-54.

The Vanishing Samaritan The Vanishing Samaritan story was recounted by well-known folklorist Richard M. Dorson in his "Negro Folktales in Michigan", pp. 129-130. The author has been unable to trace the location of Willis, Ohio.

Bill McKeon's Ghost Freeman Hubbard, "Superstitions", pp. 46-47.

The Ghostly Lovers Like many West Virginia ghost stories, this story was preserved by Ruth Ann Musick. The story may be found in her "Coffin Hollow and Other Ghost Tales", pp. 41-42.

The Phantom of Lewiston Narrows Freeman Hubbard, "Superstitions", pp. 47-48.

The White Woman of Silver Run The eerie tale of the White Woman of Silver Run Tunnel is recounted in William B. Price's "Tales and Lore of the Mountaineers" (Salem, West Virginia: Quest Publishing Company, 1963), pp. 33-38.

The Dancing Woman of Manuelito Freeman Hubbard, "Superstitions", pp. 48-49.

Battle of the Dead From Dennis William Hauck, "The National Directory of Haunted Places" (Sacramento: Athanor Press, 1994), p. 62. See also Richard Webb, "Great Ghosts of the West" (Los Angeles: Nash Publishing, 1971).

The Phantom Lantern of Ray City From John A. Burrison, editor, "Storytellers: folktales and legends from the South" (Athens, Georgia: University of Georgia Press, 1989), p. 213.

The Conductor's Ghost William (Bill) Hoke, telephone interview, Charlotte, North Carolina, July 15, 1994.

Villa Main Grade Crossing Phantoms See Dennis William Hauck, "The National Directory of Haunted Places", p. 344. Villa Main Street is located just outside of San Antonio, Texas.

Death in Georgia From Catherine Harris Ainsworth, "Folktales of America: Volume 1" (Buffalo: The Clyde Press, 1980), p. 42.

Phantom Track Layers at Sinks of Dove Creek More details about the Sinks of Dove Creek ghosts may be found in Earl Murray's "Ghosts of the Old West" (New York: Contemporary Books, 1988), pp. 109-115.

The Ghost of Doe River Gorge E. T. Campbell, "Tweetsie Tales: A Collection of Reminiscences" (Blowing Rock, North Carolina: New River Publishing Co., 1989), p. 15.

Fight on the Spur Louis C. Jones, "Things That Go Bump in the Night", pp. 147-148. The author has been unable to trace the Shenandoah & Susquehanna Railroad's history and location.

The Shake City Ghost Richard Peyton, "Journey Into Fear", p. 116.

Ghost of the New York Subway Richard Peyton, "Journey Into Fear", p. 174.

The Irishman of White Lick Creek Beth Scott and Michael Norman, "Haunted Heartland" (Madison, Wisconsin: Stanton & Lee Publishers, Inc., 1985), pp. 84-86.

The Collier Ghost Tramp You'll find versions of these stories in Ruth Ann Musick's "Coffin Hollow and Other Ghost Tales" (Lexington, Kentucky: The University Press of Kentucky, 1977), pp. 97-99. This work and her "The Telltale Lilac Bush and Other West Virginia Ghost Tales" both contain a number of fine railroad ghost stories.

Ghost Tramp of the "Cleveland Special" Ruth Ann Musick, "Coffin Hollow and Other Ghost Tales", pp. 177-179.

John Henry and Big Bend Tunnel Much information about John Henry may be found in Norm Cohen's "Long Steel Rail", pp. 61-89, and Botkin and Harlow's "A Treasury of Railroad Folklore", pp. 402-405. John Henry has also been the subject of two scholarly works and a novel, and is mentioned in virtually any general-interest history of American railroads.

The story of John Henry's ghost is from Nancy Roberts' "Appalachian Ghosts" (Garden City, New York: Doubleday & Company, Inc., 1978), pp. 37-42, and from James Gay Jones's "Haunted Valley and More Folk Tales" (Parsons, West Virginia: McClain Printing Company, 1979), p. 97.

Hoosac Tunnel Ghosts See Michael Norman and Beth Scott, "Historic Haunted America" (New York: Tom Doherty Associates, 1995), pp. 157-160.

Cowee Tunnel The Cowee Tunnel haunting first came to light in the narration used by Great Smoky Mountains Railway workers on their Dillsboro-Bryson City, North Carolina "Tuckasegee Excursion." Julie Hooper of the Great Smoky Mountains Railway was kind enough to provide the author a copy of the narration dated November 27, 1991. Additional information on the haunting was provided by Lavidge & Associates of Knoxville, Tennessee, the Great Smoky Mountains Railway's ad agency, in a press release dated December 2, 1991.

The Many Ghosts of Big Tunnel   The haunts of Big Tunnel are featured in most collections of Indiana folklore, including Linda Degh, ed., "Indiana Folklore: A Reader" (Bloomington: Indiana University Press, 1980), pp. 225-257, and Ronald L. Baker's "Hoosier Folk Legends", p. 57.

The Moonville Ghost   Robin Lacy, letter, Athens, Ohio, May 31, 1994.

Alpine Tunnel   The ghost legend is from Michael Woodill, Internet posting, June 21, 1994. Facts about the tunnel tragedy are from Dow Helmers, "Historic Alpine Tunnel" (Colorado Springs: Century One Press, 1971), pp. 54-56.

Boardtree Tunnel   Ruth Ann Musick, "The Telltale Lilac Bush and Other West Virginia Ghost Tales", pp. 122-124.

The Ghost of Grand Central   The Ghost of Grand Central comes from David Marshall's interesting 1946 book about the ex-New York Central station, "Grand Central" (New York: McGraw-Hill Book Company, Inc., 1946), pp. 58-59.

Newark Central Station   See Dennis William Hauck, "The National Directory of Haunted Places", p. 236; and Elliott O'Donnell (Harry Ludlam, editor), "Casebook of Ghosts" (Secaucus, New Jersey: Castle Books, 1989).

The Ghost of Ransomville Station   The haunting of Ransomville station is detailed in Catherine Harris Ainsworth's "Legends of New York State", p. 68.

Ghosts in the Waiting Room   Shirley Dougherty, telephone interview, Harpers Ferry, West Virginia, June 23, 1994.

Eby Witzke Returns   See Dennis William Hauck, "The National Directory of Haunted Places", p. 202; and Ruth Hein, "Ghostly Tales of Southwest Minnesota" (Fort Madison, Iowa: Quixote Press, 1989).

Denver Union Station   Dennis William Hauck, "The National Directory of Haunted Places", p. 86. Also MaryJoy Martin, "Twilight Dwellers: Ghosts, Ghouls & Goblins of Colorado" (Boulder, Colorado: Pruett Publishing, 1985). The depot is a central Beaux Arts section (built 1915) flanked by two stone wings built in 1881.

Salt Lake City Depot Ghosts   See Dennis William Hauck, "The National Directory of Haunted Places", p. 348.

Haunted "Tamalpais"/Chicago & North Western business car 400   Jim Zeirke "The ghost and car 400" "Trains", November, 1993, pp. 76-78.

Haunted Nevada Railcars   See Michael Norman and Beth Scott, "Historic Haunted America" (New York: Tom Doherty Associates, 1995), p. 219.

The Haunted Caboose   A fuller version of the haunted caboose story may be found in William F. Knapke with Freeman Hubbard's "The Railroad Caboose: Its 100 Year History, Legend and Lore" (San Marino, California: Golden West Books, 1968), pp. 175-177.

Ghost of the "Flying Yankee"   Richard Peyton, "Journey Into Fear", p. 288.

The Ghost of Glendive   Richard Peyton, "Journey Into Fear", p. 309.

Another—and very recent—legend of ghostly appearances aboard a train concerns hauntings aboard the "Spirit of Washington Dinner Train" in Renton, Washington. This Renton-to-Woodinville, Washington round trip is allegedly regularly visited by a ghost.

Locomotive 49   Stephen Hall, telephone interview, Manns Choice, Pennsylvania, June 23, 1994.

Hoodoo Engines   B. A. Botkin and Alvin F. Harlow, eds., "A Treasury of Railroad Folklore", pp. 395-398. See also Freeman Hubbard, "Superstitions", pp. 54-59. The legend of "Hoodoo" No. 571 is from Dennis William Hauck, "The National Directory of Haunted Places", p. 278. For more on Dread 107, see also Hauck, p. 87; and Mary Joy Martin, "Twilight Dwellers: Ghosts, Ghouls & Goblins of Colorado".